Discover You*th*

A Comprehensive Guide
to Equip and Inspire Adults
Who Impact Youth

BEVERLEE WENZEL

For permission requests or questions, please contact our team at:
impact@discoveryou.org
Please use the subject line: **ATTN: Discover Youth**

Published by
The ROCK Center for Youth Development
P.O. Box 2143 Midland, MI 48641

ISBN:
ISBN (Paperback): 978-1-965572-03-0
ISBN (Hardcover): 978-1-965572-01-6
ISBN (e-book): 978-1-965572-02-3

Printed in the United States of America

The stories and examples presented in *Discover You*th: *A Comprehensive Guide to Equip and Inspire Adults Who Impact Youth* are based on real-life experiences; however, names, identifying details, and certain circumstances have been altered to protect the privacy and confidentiality of the individuals involved. Any resemblance to specific persons, living or deceased, is entirely coincidental.

This book is intended for educational and inspirational purposes only. The advice and strategies provided are based on research and professional experiences, but outcomes may vary depending on individual situations. Readers are encouraged to adapt the information to their unique needs and consult professionals when necessary.

We would love to hear from you. To learn more about our programs and access resources, scan the QR code or visit this link:
https://linktr.ee/discoveryouprograms

Endorsements

"*Discover Youth* is an invaluable resource for anyone dedicated to supporting young people. Bev's genuine passion for empowering youth shines through, offering practical tools and profound insights that encourage growth, resilience, and authentic connection. These are the skills I wish I had as a 'lost' teen and young adult, and the understanding I needed to support my own children as they navigated their teenage years. As Bev says, 'Anyone with a desire and willingness can make a difference. It doesn't matter where you come from or how unlikely a candidate you seem to be for influencing youth.' This book is a gift to all who are committed to inspiring and equipping the next generation. Thank you for all that you do to make a difference in this world."

—**Leanne Camilleri,**
Owner, Reset to Thrive Australia

"I would have loved to have *Discover Youth* as a guide when I began working with young people! Beverlee Wenzel weaves compelling, relevant stories from her decades of work with young people, the wisdom of a veteran practitioner, and tested positive youth development principles into an accessible, ready-to-use tool for anyone who works with youth. It moves beyond cookie-cutter curricula to the kind of dynamic, relationship-centered, strength-based approach that meets each young person where they are and walks with them on their journeys to become their best selves."

—**Ben Houltberg,**
PhD, LMFT, President and CEO, Search Institute

"Equip, Inspire, Impact is what this book aims to achieve, and it does this and much more. A must-have resource for anybody who has a hand in shaping our youth. You start reading for the tips and tricks, you read again for the amazing stories of courage, resilience, growth, and hope that Bev has lovingly weaved through to illustrate the importance of genuine care for growing these assets in young people across the globe."

—Kylie McLerie,
School Principal, Educational Consultant, Youth Advocate, Australia

"*Discover You*th provides influential adults with tangible methods to inspire and equip generations to achieve their full potential. The process is a Tier 1 mental health support, directly combating society's many challenges. This is a must-read for everyone interacting with youth and young adults: educators, out-of-school-time professionals, parents, and community members. Increase your understanding and actively foster skills such as grit, resilience, and growth mindset in young people, creating an equitable and just society."

—George E. Kikano,
MD; Vice President for Health Affairs, CMU; Dean, Central Michigan University College of Medicine; Chairman, Central Michigan University Medical Education Partners

"Enjoy this inspiring read from a front-line expert who has taken theoretical concepts and crafted them into easy-to-implement tactics for preparing youth."

—Caroline Adams Miller,
MAPP, Author Getting Grit, Big Goals, and Creating Your Best Life

"Bev Wenzel's *Discover Youth* is a game-changer for anyone passionate about making a lasting impact on youth wellbeing. Bev masterfully distills the latest science of wellbeing into actionable, easy-to-understand concepts that make this essential knowledge accessible to everyone. This program equips adults with the skills and capabilities to foster real, sustainable, positive change in the lives of young people. Whether you're an educator, mentor, coach, or simply someone committed to supporting youth, *Discover Youth* offers practical tools to bring the science of wellbeing to life in meaningful ways. Bev's clear, insightful approach ensures that you leave with the confidence to create environments where young people can thrive. A must-read for anyone dedicated to empowering the next generation, *Discover Youth* is more than just a book—it's a blueprint for making a profound and enduring difference in the lives of the young people you serve."

—Edwina Ricci,
Director, Total Teams Australia

"An inspiring guide for youth and those who support them. This book is a remarkable gift, filled with wisdom and practical guidance that champions kindness and nurtures compassionate communities, specifically for youth. Drawing from the core frameworks of the Discover You™ Program, it authentically brings to life concepts that inspire young people to create positive change, making it an essential resource for educators, mentors, and anyone dedicated to supporting young people's growth.

With a seamless flow, it introduces the powerful 'equip, inspire, and impact' framework, alongside practical strategies for fostering resilience, wellbeing, and social and emotional learning. This book invites readers to reflect on and incorporate principles of the various frameworks, including positive psychology, within their own lives and work with youth.

A thought leader and powerhouse, Bev has crafted an empowering and authentic book as a guide that encourages young people to explore their potential and enriches our shared narrative with hope and purpose. It's a must-read for anyone looking to inspire and uplift the next generation, but an invitation for all of us to connect around our shared purpose and community. It's been a joy to read, leaving me inspired and enriched in both my work and my life!"

—Helen Gormley,
CEO and Wellbeing Coach, Helen Gormley Wellbeing,
Bath and London, United Kingdom

"In an era where the potential of our youth is both a beacon of hope and a pressing challenge, *Discover You*th emerges as an essential resource for adults dedicated to nurturing the next generation. This insightful guide, rooted in over two decades of experience in youth development, offers a powerful toolkit that empowers adults to cultivate resilience, a growth mindset, and a sense of belonging in young people.

The author's journey from leading The ROCK Center for Youth Development to creating the transformative Discover You™ program is a testament to the impact of dedicated mentorship. With over 50 practical tools and tactics, this book not only illuminates the 'how' behind youth development but also reinforces the profound belief that every young person deserves the opportunity to thrive, even amidst adversity.

Whether you are a teacher, mentor, coach, or community leader, *Discover You*th is a vital resource that invites you to reflect, engage, and take action. It inspires us to not only equip our youth with essential skills but also to cultivate our own personal growth in the process. I wholeheartedly endorse this book as a guide for anyone passionate about making a lasting impact on the lives of young people.

Together, let us champion the potential within every youth, ensuring they have the tools to not only succeed but to navigate the challenges they will face with strength and resilience."

— Janice Kershaw,
President and CEO, Brevard Schools Foundation

"Based on decades of experience in afterschool, Bev's guide provides youth workers with the encouragement needed to bolster their individual unique skills and gifts and the tools to enhance their organization's meaningful work with youth."

— Erin Skene-Pratt,
Executive Director, Michigan After School Partnership

*Discover You*th is dedicated to the youth of The ROCK and Discover You™, past, present, and future. And to all the adults who have interacted with The ROCK and Discover You™, ensuring young people have the skills to thrive when they can and struggle well when they need to.

Table of Contents

Preface

Today's youth are facing challenges that were unimaginable when I was a teen. They are continually exposed to unfiltered news of worldwide events, societal divisions are intensifying, and bullying now follows them home through their electronic devices. Families are struggling to meet their basic needs, and internal discord exacerbates the pressure. School and community resources are limited, and staff are stretched beyond their limits. The once-reliable safety nets provided by community organizations and networks are fraying as many become less engaged. Neighbors no longer know each other, and isolation is increasingly prevalent. Drug use, depression, eating disorders, and suicide are rampant among the young. All youth, regardless of status or class—those who are on the honor roll, who are loners, who are on the football team, who appear happy, whose parents give them everything they need, who seem depressed, and whose parents can't promise them dinner every night—are facing challenges. Some of these struggles are visible, while others, less so. Either way, the wellbeing of today's youth is at risk more than ever before. We can't expect someone else to fix this; it is everyone's problem to solve. But how? Where do we start? Who can help? This book helps to answer those questions.

Having led a youth organization for over twenty years, my passion for helping youth has continuously grown as I've witnessed the rising number and intensity of pressures they face. I am pleased to share in this book a model for working with youth that has been tested and proven over the years. It didn't happen overnight; it took decades of hands-on experience with youth, numerous challenges, and a great deal of hard work. When I stepped into the world of youth services, I never imagined I would someday have the experience and resulting knowledge to write this book. I didn't begin to recognize that my calling, my life's work, would be completely grounded in hope for our youth until I was in my second career.

Reaching Our Community Kids (The ROCK) was a two-year-old, fledgling nonprofit when my 14-year-old son rushed home asking me to save it. It was a local teen center that was said to be closing due to leadership concerns and a lack of funding. My son's reaction may seem dramatic, but to be fair, he was raised in rural Michigan where, by his perception, Mom saved things. Mom saved the neighbor's duck that got kicked by the horse and the dozen baby squirrels that lost their home and mother when a 40-foot oak tree dropped to the ground.

But this was different.

The ROCK had become an important part of my son's life. He was smart, curious, and rambunctious, and school wasn't his thriving place. My daughter Nichole, my son Thomas, and I had just gone through a divorce, and the fallout was still wreaking havoc on our lives. Now more than ever, safe places and good role models were a precious commodity.

Saying yes was easy when I considered how valuable The ROCK was to my son, but what I didn't know was that this journey would change me. Along the way, this effort to save The ROCK would require me to challenge societal norms and theory-to-practice models. It would demand I be innovative, bold, disruptive, and relentless. Throughout this 20-year saga, The ROCK's evolution, as well as my own, has served as the springboard for the transformation of tens of thousands of youth and thousands of adults. However, let me share a secret with you. When I started, I had no idea what I was doing or how I would do it. Through resolute dedication, vision, and the support of many amazing people, The ROCK's impact has been beyond anything I could have imagined. There aren't enough words to express the gratitude I feel when reflecting on this journey.

When I started working with The ROCK, I was a middle-level management employee and a single parent who wanted to make a positive impact in the world. I suspect you are reading this book because you, too, want to make a positive impact in the world. And like me, you see the pathway to a better world is through our youth. Let me encourage you: it doesn't matter if you are a single parent, a paraprofessional, a volunteer, an educator, or affiliated with a youth-serving organization; you have the power to impact youth in a positive way.

During our time together, I hope you examine your own unique skills, gifts, and commitment to our youth, allowing yourself to see just how well-suited you are to make a difference. The skills you explore in this book will expand your awareness and understanding of yourself as you consider your personal character strengths and mindset. Your story is uniquely yours, and that is an asset to this work. The youth you serve need you. After all, you know your kids best. You know the challenges they face and the environments in which they live. I'm just here to provide you with tools and encouragement to bolster the impact you desire to have.

In 2003, after my teenage son came home exclaiming I had to save The ROCK, I inquired about how I might help. The interim director, who was the third one in less than two years, agreed to meet me to see how I might support their work. She tasked me with reaching out to a few groups to increase awareness and garner support via volunteers or dollars. At this point, I only intended to help.

A month later, I was chatting with a board member who shared that The ROCK was in search of a permanent director. I said, "Oh," and she immediately asked if I would apply. At the time, I strongly disliked my current job and boss, so why not? Several weeks later, I was contacted for a second interview. Did I mention I never had a first interview?

On the day of the interview, I suggested to the board that they consider a different candidate. Though I was interested in the directorship, I had never operated a youth center and thought the other candidate they were considering would better serve The ROCK. I was asked to interview anyway, as they were seeking someone with a strong business background, which I had. By the time the interview began, I was enthusiastic about the role and embraced the prospective challenge, and I very much wanted a different job.

They immediately offered me the position, which entailed a significant pay cut and loss of retirement benefits and health insurance. I said I would inform them of my decision in two days. That evening, as I shared the story and offer with my partner, I said, "If it was just $2.00 more per hour, I think I could make ends meet, but this is important work, so I'm going to say yes and make up the difference somewhere else." In that moment, the phone rang, and a board member said they recognized I was taking a few days to consider the opportunity but wanted to offer an increase of $2.00 per hour to the starting salary.

Serendipity.

On my first day as The ROCK director, I drove into this vast, unmaintained, asphalt parking lot surrounded by simple country homes on large plots of land embedded in farm fields. Many of the fields touted vibrant corn stalks that towered over me, while others presented more humble plants of soybeans and sugar beets. It was a picturesque, sunny summer day with clear blue skies. The air was fresh, and there was a quiet calm as harvest time approached the Great Lakes Bay region of Michigan. In contrast to the beautiful surroundings, on the west side of the parking lot stood, in quiet disrepair, what appeared to be an abandoned church.

I had no idea what to expect as I parked the car and headed toward the building. I opened the heavy wooden doors that were unevenly hinged, causing a grating sound as they dragged across the concrete. The foyer was small and peppered with long-forgotten sweatshirts, schoolbooks, and backpacks. I came to an almost immediate and identical second set of wooden doors. As I cracked open those doors, an overwhelming smell of old pizza, sweat, and something yet to be identified engulfed me. I squinted through the darkness of the dimly lit building. I knew a lot of work would need to be done to get this program in good shape, but I was excited about the potential and immediately began imagining a center that provided a safe space for teens to just *be*. It would be a place where they could gain skills to thrive as individuals, a space where they could navigate the struggles of life. The center would be a resource for teens to find support to meet their basic needs, all while surrounded by caring adults who could hold tight to high expectations, ensure accountability, and provide safety nets.

But in that moment, I needed to find a light switch. I walked behind the unmanned welcome desk toward the little natural light making its way into this mammoth building. That light led me to an office where I was greeted by a pseudo-Clint Eastwood voice attempting to mask his youth: "I'm Bob, head of security here. You must be Bev." He leaned back in the black office chair as aged as the building, folded his hands behind his head, put his feet on the peeling Formica desk, and, in full character, placed a toothpick in his mouth.

The neglected building, combined with Bob's territorial behavior, gave me the sense that I'd just entered *Lord of the Flies* and was likely face-to-face with my first nemesis. As I'm sure was Bob's plan, he needed to establish two rules upfront: ensure your opponent knows you're serious and take your position. A manila folder with my name on it caught my eye. I looked Bob square in the eye and said, "Hey Bob, get your feet off my desk."

Bob slowly stood up and said, "Well, let me show you around."

During my Bob-orientation, it was revealed he had just finished middle school. I quickly came to realize Bob loved The ROCK and took both ownership and responsibility for it. He was, after all, the most consistent presence between the two of us, with me being the fourth director he had taken upon himself to orient. I decided I could not and would not disappoint Bob or my son. There was no way I would allow The ROCK to fail on my watch.

Over 20 years later, the vision and dream of The ROCK are alive and well. There is Discover You™, more ROCK out-of-school-time locations, more youth, more programs, and every young person reaching their potential remains our north star. My enthusiasm has never waned through this time because I found my passion and purpose inside those doors. We have healthy places where youth are provided with skills, opportunities, and boundaries to grow within, just like I envisioned from the first day. The initial vision is now a reality and will continue through you.

I suspect you are reading this book because you want to realize your own vision for your youth. It is my honor to be able to support you in that pursuit, and I look forward to hearing how this book, combined with the concepts and tools shared within, will aid you in your efforts. Just like The ROCK, your process will likely be a journey of trial and error, success, and seeming failure. Along the way, hold close the idea that every moment and every imprint you make matters. Be it with one youth or hundreds.

As you go through your journey, I enthusiastically welcome you to share your stories of success and how implementing the practices in this book helped you. Send an email to impact@discoveryou.org anytime. Our team cannot wait to hear about your moments, both big and seemingly small.

Note to Reader

This book is intended as a guide and perhaps a touch of encouragement. I will demonstrate how I began this journey as someone who felt unqualified but who learned along the way that I was just the right person to do this impactful work. Through reading our story, you will know with absolute certainty that you can and will have a great impression on our youth, regardless of your perceived qualifications.

The names of individuals, programs, and organizations have been changed to protect the innocent and the guilty. Creative liberty has been taken in events, and while I may use "you," I am referring to all of us. There is much truth to the idea that there is no original idea or thought, as we truly are a collective.

I have learned from authors, researchers, experts, laypeople, young children, teens, teachers, out-of-school-time professionals, and others in my life. It is my sincere desire to celebrate and recognize each and every one of you and accurately cite your work. Inevitably, I have missed someone. Should that be you, please accept my apologies and notify me so we can correct that and recognize you.

Lastly, this work is a derivative of front-line efforts; it is the application of concepts and is intended to provide ideas and considerations. At no point is this work intended to diagnose or prescribe. If you have concerns, please seek professional support as needed. I cite research and authors throughout, but do not consider myself an expert. The examples used reflect my team's and my own successful or unsuccessful application of these concepts. Your outcomes and those of the youth you influence will vary and should not be expected to replicate ours.

Throughout this book, you will find stories to entertain and provide context, definitions, and explanations. And I will convince and assure you our youth's future is in your capable hands. I look forward to you joining me, as it will take every one of us to help this generation develop the tools they need to succeed.

This book is divided into three parts: 1) Hope. Strength. Resilience. 2) Courage. Confidence. Connection. 3) Purpose. Motivation. Intention. Although the concepts are organized with a specific strategy in mind for mastery, they often intertwine and build upon one another.

Discover Youth encompasses over 50 concepts and skills, aiming to be both extensive and comprehensive, but not exhaustive. I hope you enjoy the book in its entirety and that it provides you with multiple "ah-ha" moments. After that, I encourage you to use it as a reference book to support you in specific situations and as needed. At the end of each chapter is an application section called Equip • Inspire • Impact, with quick tips to help you easily and immediately implement tactics.

The concepts in *Discover Youth* can be integrated throughout your existing work and programs. You can teach and apply these tools in any class, such as leadership, social sciences, health, or science. As an administrator, you can equip educators and support staff, including those in transportation, food service, administration, and paraprofessional roles. If your focus is on out-of-school-time, these skills can be easily integrated into after-school programs, sports, clubs, or youth groups. As a parent, I can't say enough about the immediate and long-term benefits you will create for your home and child.

I hope you enjoy our time together as much as I have enjoyed compiling our story.

Introduction

"A journey of a thousand miles begins with a single step."
— *Chinese Proverb*

Life is a dichotomy. A beautiful and often frustrating blend of opportunities and challenges, good and bad, hope and despair. Youth and adults alike face challenges in life. Whether at school, work, or home, we inevitably encounter difficulties that push our strength and determination to the limit at some point. It's also true that some of us experience significantly more struggles than others. Despite the nuances of life's challenges and the many disparities that exacerbate them, with the right set of tools and skills, our ability to triumph increases exponentially.

The challenges of today disproportionately impact our youth, and our youth are carrying a lot. When I started at The ROCK, I knew my team needed to create something new if we were going to give the youth we were serving an opportunity to create a quality life for themselves. Even if the methods weren't new, we would need to create a disruptive combination of tactics to develop into proven practices that would create measurable change. Although I did not have this language or clarity on how to proceed at the beginning of this journey, I had a deep desire to first understand the gaps that were creating the greatest obstacles for the youth in our program. I also needed to better understand the surrounding systems.

On one of my first days at The ROCK, I encountered a young man named Charles. Whenever I saw Charles, he'd be sitting in the same spot and always alone. Other youth would try to interact with him, to include him, but he'd stay back and remain disengaged. It tugged at my heart every time I saw him and snuck into my mind when I was in a reflective space.

The nagging questions varied: How can I help Charles help himself? What is wrong in Charles's world? Was there a problem with his home life or at school? Did someone do something to him? My initial observations led me to the conclusion that someone should be doing something. In retrospect, I realize that this was one of the many gaps and disconnects that fueled my development of both The ROCK and Discover You™.

Seeing Charles in that way broke my heart. As I forged ahead, I let the image of Charles and many like him stay at the forefront of my mind. You have likely encountered at least one Charles. A young person who evokes a strong desire in you to support them, motivating you to take action. In our individual efforts, we know firsthand that our young people need fundamental tools. We want them to develop age-appropriate resilience and showcase a growth mindset. Within safe boundaries, we want them to be able to make mistakes and to be able to fail well, as they learn to make responsible choices.

As I sought solutions, I would hear others speak on the topics, learn of a related book or curriculum, and rush to investigate it. What I generally found was that their mindset and intentions were similar to mine. They recognized that our youth needed these competencies, and they understood that adults also required similar skills. Most of my preliminary findings were self-help books that carried the message, "If I can do it, so can you." But they were always theoretical.

The books lacked the tactical. They never shared the "how," and they left me, the reader, trying to figure out how to reach my goal. The message was empowering on the surface, but honestly, I would close the book with a brief burst of enthusiasm, only to be discouraged all over again. Deflated, I became overwhelmed by this massive conundrum of trying to serve our youth without possessing a sound and actionable plan.

After seeing me struggle in my search and learning of my frustration, a friend advised me to create the program and processes I sought. More than once, she pointed out that the vision for a strength-based, experiential approach to youth development had the potential for great impact, but I dismissed her because I didn't believe I was qualified. Oh sure, I had a certain understanding and pretty good instincts, but I didn't have the letters behind my name to say I was sufficiently credentialed to solve the problem. That being my seventh year at The ROCK, I had interacted with thousands of teens, both personally and professionally, and still wasn't sure I had enough experience with youth to undertake such an endeavor. Eventually, out of sheer desperation and reckless abandon, I warmed up to the idea of giving it a try.

Throughout, doubt surfaced as I questioned, *Who did I think I was to take on this issue and address the greatest, ever-growing problem of a generation?* Uncertainty prevails as I remain unsure who is qualified to do this important work and who gets to change the world. Though indeed someone else is more qualified than I, some clarity presented itself during the process. And of this, I am certain: someone needs to do it, or it won't get done. That's where you and I come in. Regardless of our personal and professional circumstances, we show up to do the work. For me, it was creating a program under The ROCK umbrella called Discover You™. Now,

I am ready to expand the positive impact of that work by sharing what I have learned with you.

Welcome to *Discover Youth*.

Opportunities

"Within our dreams and aspirations,
we find opportunities."

— *Sugar Ray Leonard*

Imagine a world where all youth have the opportunity to live their potential. Visualize communities where strengths are leveraged, where youth live their passions and purpose, and where benevolence prevails. For a moment, pause, and just imagine…

Our young people are not a problem to be solved, but a treasure to be unveiled and a positive force to be unleashed. In every young person, possibilities abound, and solutions to societal challenges await discovery.

"Thrive when you can and struggle well when you need to" is a phrase coined by Discover You™ to demonstrate the universal value of the competencies and skills we promote for youth. The skills one needs to thrive are the same as those needed to struggle well.

To thrive is to flourish or prosper; it is to be in a desired state of optimal functioning. And although we all prefer to thrive, we often find ourselves in a state of struggle when life becomes more difficult and challenges are prevalent. As struggles are to be expected in this life, youth need to have the skills to struggle well, identify problems and persist through them, find solutions, and fail well. These abilities can support their journey through the challenges, leading our youth toward success.

Providing young people with these resources as early as possible allows them to develop and build on those skills daily, drawing on them as situations arise throughout their lives. The diverse application of these competencies is why they are critical and appropriate for both youth who demonstrate the highest levels of functioning and those who appear to have extreme challenges and limitations.

> Thrive when you can and struggle well when you need to.

At Discover You™, we recognize that out-of-school-time (OST) professionals, parents, and educators alike routinely face seemingly insurmountable challenges. We continue to sit with you in the trenches of real-life applied work. You and I do not live in a theoretical world where problems are solved on paper. We live in a world where hunger is real, guardians are incarcerated, imposed expectations can be ridiculously high or insanely non-existent, substance misuse takes precedence over children, and bureaucracy abounds and inhibits.

As you experience *Discover Youth*, you will find that you inevitably apply the concepts to yourself first, as these are foundational constructs that all of humanity needs. And more than in any other arena, the youth need you to possess, model, and embrace the skills first. Our youth need you to be strong and resilient, embody a growth mindset, and be healthy risk-takers. You will be hard-pressed to find a component in the book that doesn't speak to you personally and in every aspect of your world. Adults who develop this knowledge through our Discover You™ program tell us they become better educators, OST professionals, youth workers, parents, aunts, uncles, coaches, and coworkers. They become better humans.

While you integrate the concepts into your own life, you will share them with the youth in your world. Sometimes, this happens when modeling the behaviors you have learned. Other times, you will be more explicit in teaching skills to young people in a formal or informal setting. Perhaps you can discuss them, ask thought-provoking questions, or create a space for the youth to explore their ideas. Whatever your combination of tactics, you will witness your personal growth positively impacting the young people around you.

PART I

Hope. Strength. Resilience.

Hope. Strength. Resilience.

*"You never know how strong you are
until strong is your only choice."*

— *Bob Marley*

It was 86 degrees with humidity to match. It might have been cooler in the shade if there had been any, but there wasn't. There wasn't much of anything except fields surrounding The ROCK, an unassuming rural teen center. It was late afternoon, mid-July, and the center was open for drop-ins. Providing drop-in hours at The ROCK began after we realized that scheduled programs didn't address the entirety of the needs of our participants. Many of our youth lacked good options to fill their days during school breaks, which could put them at risk of engaging in less-than-productive activities. We recognized that more needed to be done outside of regular hours, so we introduced the drop-in option.

The ROCK would open from 8 a.m. to 6 p.m., Monday through Thursday, and 12 p.m. to 10 p.m. on Fridays in the summer. It became a safe place for kids to come to when they needed it. For parents, we were a trusted resource, providing supportive adults who could care for their teens as they worked or just get them active outside the home. Some of our youth sought out drop-ins on their own, coming to us on bikes or getting rides from their parents or guardians. So far, there weren't any takers on this smoldering summer afternoon. The ever-busy, lean staff went about their day, working on the tasks that kept the business side of The ROCK running smoothly. Some were doing inventory, another group worked on summer programs, and one was mowing the grass.

Paula, our Administrative Assistant, was busy paying bills when she heard the door open. She saw two of our youth and said, "Oh, hey, Jess and Beth. I haven't seen you all summer."

"Hi Paula," responded Jess, the taller of the two sisters. Jess was 14 and always carried a serious air about her. Beth was 12 and appeared generally unsure of herself. Today, Beth's long brunette hair was tucked precariously into a stocking cap.

"How did you get here?" asked Paula, making conversation.

"We walked," chimed in Beth, sporting a red face and appearing exhausted.

"Don't you live like four miles from here?" asked Paula. The rural roads surrounding The ROCK had no sidewalks or shoulders for safe foot travel, especially when cars sped down them. Traffic accidents were rare, but when they occurred, they were generally serious.

"Six, actually," said Jess.

"Come on, let's get you a drink. Are you hungry?" asked Paula. She knew they were hungry; teens are always hungry. Plus, most teens aren't ambitious enough to walk six miles in 86-degree heat with a stocking cap on.

"Yes!" responded Beth. "We're starving. And dying of thirst. Can we have a soda?"

"Let's get you water first before you faint," suggested Paula.

The three left the low-lit office area to move toward The ROCK's Cafe. The ROCK's budget had always been tight, stretching resources thin. However, we had always been adamant about keeping a well-stocked kitchen with a variety of options that our youth enjoyed. We knew meals weren't guaranteed for all of them, so we made sure that whenever they might need or want something to eat, they knew they could always come to us without money, shame, or judgment.

As Paula searched for food options for the sisters, she suspected that the girls had made the gruesome trek because something was amiss. She kept her concern to herself as she handed them each a bottle of water and asked, "How about grilled cheese sandwiches?"

"That's our favorite!" squealed Beth.

Jess joined Paula in the kitchen. "Can I help?"

"Sure, grab the bread from over there," Paula suggested. "And tell me what's going on with you and your sister."

"It's nothing. We just needed to get out of the house," Jess whispered.

Paula saw Jess's willingness to help as an opportunity to begin the conversation they needed to have. As they stood shoulder to shoulder at the counter, she implored, "Jess, tell me what's going on with you and your sister." There was no response from Jess. "Jess, if you tell me the whole story, maybe I can help," Paula replied, flipping the sandwiches on the grill nonchalantly. She was making five. Two for each of the girls and one for her. Paula knew, as you and I do, that shared mealtimes are an ideal opportunity for bonding. Sitting down together at a table helps youth feel safe as the elements of trust and togetherness culminate. The simple act of having a meal together builds and binds humanity. Paula didn't watch the girls eat or ask questions from a standardized form; instead, she created a safe space to participate in a tough conversation by sharing a meal.

Paula's strategy proved successful as the three sat at a cafe table and enjoyed their grilled cheese sandwiches, chips, and sodas.

"We just had to get out of the house and hoped someone was

here. We're glad it was you." Jess smiled hesitantly as she glanced at Paula.

At the center, Paula was one of our teen favorites. That might seem odd as she was a back-of-the-house staff member, but that never mattered at our center. Our leadership team had worked hard to empower each of our staff members at every level to be an agent of change for our youth, regardless of their job, appearance, background, or personality. Organizationally, we had a policy that every door was open, and every adult received training so they felt comfortable supporting our teens and could easily leverage any opportunity to build connections. What we could not teach was the desire to do good for youth. Thus, we were intentional about hiring adults who wanted to be there for the right reason, and that reason was the youth, pure and simple.

I believe that is one of the key components of the impact we have had on numerous lives. That's one of the many reasons why, despite Paula's gruff exterior, kids were drawn to her warm, caring nature and her tell-it-how-it-is approach. She was that adult who always welcomed them, never sugarcoated anything, sincerely listened, and provided treats. For them, Paula was safe. "Tell me more" was Paula's simple response.

"We were hungry," replied Beth, well into her second sandwich. Jess looked at Beth and affectionately rubbed her head.

"You want half my sandwich? I guess I'm not that hungry," Paula asked Beth.

Beth reached out for Paula's sandwich.

Paula continued to search for answers thoughtfully. "And what's up with the stocking cap? It's a little warm for one, isn't it? Though I must say, it looks great on you." Jess and Beth looked at each other for a long moment, and then Jess gently pulled off Beth's hat. Small stubs of chopped hair replaced her beautiful, brown, shoulder-length locks.

"I'm listening," Paula said intently, not appearing bothered by what she saw.

"Mom cut my hair off this morning. I said I was dressed, but my hair was still messy. Mom grabbed scissors and cut it all off." Beth was on the verge of tears as she spoke.

"Things aren't good at our house," said Jess. "And we aren't going back."

Paula was confident that the haircut was possibly the last straw, but it was far from the only problem. She and the other staff had thought something was off whenever they observed the sisters, but had never been certain.

Paula's mind raced as she weighed the implications of this situation. Instinctually, Paula was very maternal. She wanted to protect the sisters, but professionally, she knew there was more to consider, such as navigating Child Services. To add another layer of complexity, Paula wanted to help while maintaining the trust of Jess and Beth. It can be particularly challenging when dealing with youth who need and want help but are struggling with their rightful connection to their current environment and families. The situation was delicate and multilayered. Paula was certain that if her actions caused the girls to feel betrayed, she would lose not only today's but also any future opportunity to help them. She decided it was best to partner with the sisters, allowing them to maintain a sense of control over their own lives and build a solution together.

"Who do you trust that we can call?" was Paula's first question. When the sisters couldn't readily provide the name of a trusted adult, Paula thought it might be that the girls simply didn't want to involve other family members. But because they had walked six miles to The ROCK, Paula considered that perhaps there were no other adults they trusted. Families are complex, and often, when one adult is neglecting or abusing their children, the family dynamics become extremely messy. Still, doing her due diligence and taking the proper steps meant asking the question.

The entire predicament put Paula and The ROCK in a vulnerable position. We always want to honor the family first. However, under the Michigan Child Protection Law, it is our legal responsibility to report any known or suspected harm to children to the authorities to protect these kids. Beyond what is legally required in our profession, The ROCK staff holds what is ethically and morally right in high regard. In our roles, these two commitments occasionally feel in conflict, especially in circumstances where family members who should be providing protection are the ones inflicting harm.

Paula listened as the girls shared their circumstances. Beth's haircutting experience involved Mom throwing her on the floor, Mom's boyfriend holding her down, and Mom aggressively chopping off her hair. With the most minor infraction, the girls would be locked in their rooms. Food was routinely in a padlocked cabinet to which only Mom and her boyfriend had access, and was withheld as a form of punishment. The ugly list of the atrocities these young women were enduring continued. After Paula gathered this information, she called me. Together, we evaluated options and alternatives for Jess and Beth's situation.

"I'm not letting them go home," Paula declared like the protector she was.

"Of course not," I replied as calmly as I could, recognizing that the decision was not ours to make. Keeping my rage at bay and knowing full well that expertly managing our emotions was what we'd have to do. It was not the time to respond quickly or erratically. "What are our options?" At that point, I had been working with teens for about five years. My goal is always to make the best choice, which often requires sorting through intricacies and nuances of lives that aren't mine to meddle in. Eventually, the best choice always presents itself, but it's not an easy process.

To achieve the best possible outcome, I leverage the 5 I's Model, which we created to remind staff of the critical steps involved in managing challenging situations: **Incident**, **Investigate**, **Ideate**, **Implement**, and **Inform**.

Incident: The event that triggers a response.

The sisters sharing the circumstances of their unsafe home environment triggered a response from ROCK staff.

Investigate: The process of gathering as much information as possible.

First, I gathered and considered the facts: Mom was the legal guardian, meaning the girls had to go home. In the past, Grandma and Aunt had asked not to be involved. With one call from us, Child Protective Services would likely investigate, and the police would conduct a welfare check.

Ideate: The process of weighing the information and developing the best possible plan of action.

Shelters in our county won't accept minors without adult guardians. The closest safe place for minors without adults is two counties south. If we transported the girls out of the county, we could be charged with kidnapping. If Paula or any staff housed the girls, the list of criminal charges could be staggering. It was getting late in the day when I considered an immediate viable solution, which came down to keeping The ROCK open so the sisters could stay. We could operate the center during any hours we choose, which temporarily addressed many of the potential problems.

Implement: The implementation of the plan.

We kept the center open and began taking the necessary steps to ensure the girls' safety.

After a long period of silence, Jess said with a hint of desperation, "I think we should just call Grandma and Aunt Ness. Maybe they will come. They're great. Just tired of all of this. They tried to help us before, but Mom makes it so difficult every time."

"How about I call them with you?" suggested Paula.

A typical day of bookkeeping and administration turned into a pivotal day in the lives of two sisters. Though Grandma and Aunt Ness had chosen not to be involved in the past, today they came to help the girls. They expressed that they were now ready to take legal action to permanently become the sisters' legal guardians. Due to the involvement of The ROCK, they felt supported. Grandma and Aunt Ness decided to keep the sisters together and have them alternate between their homes until the situation was resolved.

Inform: This step involves informing appropriate parties, such as parents, authorities, and supervisors, and documenting the information as needed or required.

Child Protective Services was notified, as were the police. Incident reports were completed. Investigations ensued, charges were filed, and, to my knowledge, the sisters never returned to their unsafe home environment.

From that point, whenever the girls came into the center, we'd do quick and casual check-ins and exchange knowing glances. In such a situation, the key is to provide young people with opportunities for conversation without applying pressure to speak or drawing attention to them in front of their peers. Should everything continue to improve for the sisters, they knew who we were and where we were if they needed us for anything again.

Paula or I would also make it a point to discreetly take the sisters aside and ask how they were doing. We didn't want to assume that because of one intervention, the entire situation was resolved. Experience tells us that occasionally, unsafe situations escalate after third parties are involved. Unless we checked in with the girls, we likely wouldn't know if they returned to an unsafe environment or if their current situation was any better. Jess and Beth's story exemplifies the concepts of Hope. Strength. Resilience.

Hope abounded when the sisters took the first step in the six-mile walk to the center. They were hopeful that someone would be at The ROCK and that the right person might be able to help, even if they didn't know the specific help they needed.

Strength prevailed as Jess and Beth stood up every day and faced the challenges life provided them. They remained strong through their predicament and persisted in seeking solutions within their community despite the obstacles and risks they faced.

Resilience rang loud as the girls endured stressful and traumatic circumstances. Throughout, Jess and Beth consistently demonstrated their determination to tackle their challenges and create a better way forward for themselves and each other.

Chapter 1

Hope

"May your choices reflect your hopes, not your fears."
— *Nelson Mandela*

"Hope" is a verb and a noun, a state, and an action. As a verb, "hope" is a vision reflecting a desired future supported by action and understanding. As a noun, it is an expectation of a desired state where things will turn out for the best. The best is not necessarily perfect, just the best it can be.

In her book *Atlas of the Heart*, researcher and author Brené Brown describes hope as a function of struggle that is developed in adverse and uncomfortable circumstances. A lack of hope yields hopelessness and despair.

The mission of The ROCK is to build hope and resilience in youth based on a foundation of acceptance, support, and respect. Hope and resilience. I use those words often because when our youth possess those two attributes, they have the basic tools to face another day.

Hope is different from optimism. Optimism is a way of thinking that anticipates the best possible outcome. If unchecked, it is a mindset that can lead to making assumptions for the best and disregarding the efforts often required to achieve those outcomes. Optimism is a good thing when grounded in realism.

Hope is a function that requires specific components, including vision, agency, and pathways. Hope is the agent of change. It is the catalyst that inspires us or the state that causes us to look to a preferred future. Hope first requires a vision or a goal and helps to move us toward something in the future. Vision + Pathways + Agency = Hope. We can hope for the night to end and the sun to rise, for the birth of a baby or a better-paying job. For our young people, their hopes may be to make friends, earn a passing grade, learn to drive, or escape an awful situation.

A good example of hope is Nina. Discover You™ staff visit Lincoln High School weekly throughout the school year. Leveraging the health class, all ninth-grade

> Hope is a nearly limitless inner resource that harnesses strength and creates the future we want to live in.

students participate in a series of Discover You™ workshops. Through the interactive program, youth learn to understand and apply concepts such as character strengths, resilience, team building, growth mindset, forgiveness, and gratitude. Upon completion of the Discover You™ program, Nina wrote, "Thank you for coming every week. I now have hope." This comment intrigued me, as hope in itself has sustained me most of my life.

When I asked her if she cared to tell me more, Nina shared how she had all but given up on everything. Her mother was an addict, and she hadn't seen her father since elementary school. She was responsible for caring for her younger sister and often lacked the necessary resources to provide for the two of them. Through the "Knowing What I Know" exercise, a process in which students learn about self-efficacy and how to transfer successes or lessons learned from one area of their life to a different challenge, she understood how much more she was capable of, based on her past wins. That exercise, paired with many of the other 40+ skills she had explored in Discover You™, helped Nina understand she could have a vision of the future and that she possessed the capacity to work toward it. She now had hope, and with this hope, she could continue the fight.

Hope requires agency, which is one's personal motivation to move toward the future. There is personal responsibility in hope due to the required motivation, which is discussed in more depth in Chapter 8. Nina needed motivation to move toward her future to feel hopeful, and her younger sister's wellbeing was her motivation.

When young people have hope, they become more invested in finding pathways to achieve their goals or, at the very least, believe that attainable pathways exist. When one feels hopeless, it can manifest itself in the present day as well as in a future vision. The lack of hope can diminish motivation in youth's daily lives, affecting relationships, academics, and engagement. This is often because they don't see a future, cannot envision a path or means to achieve it, and/or don't believe in their ability to reach that future. Hope is a nearly limitless inner resource that harnesses strength and creates the future we want to live in.

Hope is a powerful tool for adults as well. As I mentioned earlier, hope has sustained me for most of my life and influenced our work. The ROCK and Discover You™ are excellent examples of the power of hope. The vision we hold tight to is for all youth to have the opportunity to live their potential. Our staff, like many, work with young people daily, often in challenging situations. Like other youth-serving professionals, they appear to harbor a deep-seated belief in the potential for positive outcomes for youth. Even in the face of challenges, they remain hopeful because they are empowered with all the components of hope. The pathway is clear, as their knowledge and acquired skills, gained through our training, equip them to implement the Discover You™ programs. They also possess the autonomy to contribute to the development of the program as directed by the changing landscape for youth. By design of the profession they chose, they hold the agency, or motivation, if you will, to work toward hope. In other words, they believe in the work and the concepts, have seen the wins and the outcomes, and are empowered to reach for their vision of youth living up to their potential.

An excellent resource on hope is the Hope Scale, created by C.R. Snyder. This free online tool helps measure and better understand hope. This 12-item scale allows you to evaluate your agency and pathway levels of hope using a 1-8 ranking.

Like most concepts discussed throughout this book, we can combine various skills, competencies, behaviors, and knowledge to increase hope. The following sections focus on strong hope builders, including a growth mindset, positive emotions, gratitude, and reframing thoughts.

Equip · Inspire · Impact

- **Encourage young people to develop hope by defining their future vision.**
- **Assist the continued development of hope in young people by helping them identify the path or steps they will take to achieve that future.**
- **Equip young people with the third component of hope by ensuring they understand their motivation and why achieving said goal is important to them.**

Growth Mindset

"She believed she could, so she did."
— *R.S. Grey*

Carol Dweck, Ph.D., a leading researcher and author of the book Mindset: The New Psychology of Success, states that you choose your mindset, which is simply powerful beliefs. A growth mindset is open and provides opportunity; it revels in growth and change.

A person with a growth mindset:

- Believes qualities, abilities, and characteristics can be cultivated, changed, and grown through their efforts
- Views traits as a starting point, not simply a hand they're dealt and must live with
- Demonstrates a passion for learning and growing
- Sees the process as part of the journey
- Values effort
- Views failure as an opportunity for growth

Young people with a growth mindset are generally eager to learn, take healthy risks, exhibit greater resilience, and tend to persevere. They do not let mistakes define them and often thrive in the face of challenges. This is not to imply that having a growth mindset means that one does not encounter and endure difficulties. Obstacles will arise, regardless of our mindset. The key difference is that a person with a growth mindset confronts and overcomes these obstacles. They may feel discouraged and disappointed, but they don't give up.

Now, let's compare that to its rival, a fixed mindset. When we think of fixed or deficit-based mindsets, we think of being stuck, of believing your qualities are carved in stone.

A person with a fixed mindset:

- Views intelligence as static
- Feels threatened by the success of others
- Believes things can't change
- Strives for success and continual validation
- Views effort as bad
- Thinks errors mean incompetence
- Avoids failure at all costs

Young people who struggle with a fixed mindset often need to look smart, leading them to avoid challenges, give up easily when faced with obstacles, view efforts as fruitless or too much work, ignore constructive feedback, and only thrive when assured of success.

To demonstrate, consider the time Bella faced challenges in math class. "I'm not good at math," declared Bella, a sixth-grade student, as she tossed her homework on Ms. Alice's desk. The bell rang to signal the end of the day, and the other students hurried off to their after-school activities. Ms. Alice looked at the failing mark and recalled grading the paper. She knew Bella was struggling in her class.

"We can work together an extra hour or two a week, and I can help you," Ms. Alice suggested. She was trained in Discover You™ and familiar with tactics to increase a growth mindset.

"It won't do any good. I told you I'm no good at math," Bella declared. In that moment, she created a future in which she'd never see herself doing well in math. Ms. Alice cringed as history told her Bella would likely labor all year, ultimately failing the class. Math consists of required courses that continually build on skills from previous lessons. Not only would Bella's current academic year be hampered by her dislike of math, but she would likely struggle with all math-based subjects in the future as she would lack a solid foundation.

We all have young people in our lives like Bella. We may ask ourselves, what influenced their mindset? How do you help the Bellas broaden their worldview? An important first step is to help our youth recognize that they choose their mindset and can change it. A young person's mindset impacts every decision they make and every risk they are willing to take, influencing the opinions they hold and all their relationships. A young person's mindset is their world, and adopting a growth mindset is one of the most critical choices they will make.

The effects of a fixed mindset, as Bella demonstrated, persist throughout a person's life and can be substantially limiting in many areas. Consider the young person who appears successful. They get to college, and what was once easy is now difficult, and they begin to doubt themselves. What happened to them? If they possess a fixed mindset, they may have learned their whole lives that they were smart, but now, suddenly, they don't feel smart. It doesn't come as easily. It's hard, so this must mean they are not smart; they only thought they were smart. They begin to think they aren't capable and aren't suited for university or post-secondary opportunities. This often happens because the fixed mindset they developed led them to believe that intelligence was natural and didn't require effort. When it got difficult, they gave up.

Compare that to a young person who learned in their early

years that they needed to put in effort to get good grades, they can do hard things, and it is fine to fail. Essentially, they possess a solid growth mindset, enabling them to adapt to challenges and overcome difficulties throughout their academic journey and beyond. Their likelihood of success is exponentially greater due to their growth mindset.

When this student experiences increasingly difficult challenges in postsecondary education, they are not surprised. They expected the challenge and look forward to putting forth effort to learn. They lean into the experience. When they encounter obstacles, they seek resources and support, and struggle well when they need to.

> A young person's mindset is their world, and adopting a growth mindset is one of the most critical choices they will make.

Most people have both a fixed and a growth mindset, often in the same situation. Consider how one might have a fixed mindset about math but a growth mindset about English. As a caring adult, you can teach and model the value of effort and development. Something as simple as adding the word "yet." The word "yet" states that something is in progress, that we are still working on it. "I'm not good at sports, yet." Those three letters open the world to possibilities of learning and growth.

One of the greatest attributes of out-of-school-time (OST) is growth, which can be celebrated without the need to assign grades based on performance relative to right or wrong. OST can be a powerful arena to help young people learn to embrace mistakes, take risks, and view failing as a vessel for improvement. ROCK OST focuses on the process, not the outcome. The fun and point are in the experience or the doing. Every attempt to make a nameplate using a 3D printer is an improvement in developing a skill, not a failure.

If a young person gets 40% of the questions on a science test wrong, they are traditionally graded as failing. However, that person got 60% right, which is perhaps twice as many correct answers as they got last time. When viewed through the lens of significant growth, this is both encouraging and empowering. When viewed through the lens of a failed grade, it is, well, failure on top of failure.

Mindsets require balance, and it can be easy to flip from a critical approach to a "you are great because you are" approach. Despite being well-intentioned, the idea that everyone gets a trophy and everyone wins can undermine many opportunities for personal development, including a growth mindset. When winning comes from effort, not just showing up, it increases the likelihood that one will increase efforts relative to increased challenges. The "you are great because you are" concept can create a false sense of self-esteem that isn't founded on the hard work and effort required to be in many situations.

Children benefit from adults who lead with a growth mindset and employ a variety of tactics to stimulate curiosity, development, and learning. Those adults might set lofty goals and then educate youth on how to achieve them. In contrast, adults with a fixed mindset might unintentionally limit growth by focusing on the young person's intelligence and giftedness, perpetuating a "do not fail" mentality.

As trusted adults, your priority should be fostering growth mindsets in youth. The ability for young people to grow foundationally lies in their belief that they can grow. Avoid labeling mistakes; instead, lean into constructive learning and focus on building skills and knowledge. Bella's teacher could take the opportunity to show Bella everything she got correct on her math test. Ms. Alice might consider circling correct answers and talking through those. Perhaps the opportunity would arise for Ms. Alice to demonstrate how one correct answer might lead to correcting a different, incorrect one. She could also celebrate with Bella the knowledge Bella possesses that didn't show up on the test. This approach is helpful in redirecting the focus toward developing the skill (learning) instead of on the end product (grade).

Next, consider how we can help young people to improve their outcomes by intervening at the thought level. We will demonstrate the often-subconscious process we mentally go through considering **Circumstance, Thoughts, Action,** and **Outcomes.**

> **Circumstance:** First, consider the circumstance. Something happens.
>
> **Thoughts:** Next, there are thoughts or mindsets about what happened. This is where either a fixed or a growth mindset occurs.
>
> **Action:** Then, an action is taken based on the person's mindset or belief about what is happening.
>
> **Outcomes:** Finally, there are actual outcomes or consequences resulting from their actions.

All of this determines or reinforces a young person's self-perception, or how they see themselves and their abilities.

We will use a path analogy to demonstrate to Bella how her chosen mindset affects her outcomes. Bella has a pending math test, which is the current circumstance, bringing her to a fork in the path. The path to the right represents the growth mindset path, and the path to the left represents the fixed mindset path. Along each path lay opportunities, one labeled as thought, the next as action, and ending with outcomes.

Bella is facing a math test with two possible outcomes: one that leverages a growth mindset and the other a fixed mindset.

Bella begins down the fixed mindset path, thinking, "I'm not good at math." "The teacher doesn't like me." "I'll look stupid." "Why should I study? I'll fail anyway." The teacher won't help me."

Next, she arrives at action. Based on her thoughts, Bella acts like it doesn't matter, so her actions are to go to a friend's house and not waste her time studying for something at which she believes she will fail.

Bella then arrives at the outcome of having failed the test, which validates her beliefs. She now has the reinforced self-perception that she was right: she is not good at math, and it isn't worth the effort.

Return to the fork in the path, where this time Bella decides to try the growth mindset option. Here, her thoughts are, "I may not be good at math yet, but I can learn." "It's okay if I don't get it all right this time. I can keep trying." "I will study and get better." "I can ask the teacher for help."

Next, Bella arrives at the point of action: she studies an extra hour per day and asks the teacher for help.

Bella reaches the outcome, having experienced growth in math, which validates her ability to learn and do hard things. She has now built the self-perception that she can learn and grow, and investing time and effort pays off.

Dweck addresses the influence of adults on how young people view themselves. Dweck explains that adults can convey either a fixed mindset message, emphasizing that traits are permanent, or a growth mindset message, asserting that they are in a continual state of development and growth.

When you interact with youth, remember that many words and actions convey a fixed or growth mindset attitude. The type of messages you send to youth can influence, if not define, the mindset they have. Back to the classroom, where Bella was giving up on math. Her new response is, "I'm not good at math yet, but I'm working on it."

Mindset will bring our youth to the top. Skills alone aren't enough. Mindset is everything, so encourage young people to choose their mindset wisely. As a caring adult, consider how you can support a growth mindset whenever possible.

Equip · Inspire · Impact

- **Focus on fostering a growth mindset by emphasizing hard work over being naturally smart.**
- **Add the word "yet" when discussing areas in the development process.**
- **Use a real-life example and compare the outcomes as they relate to engaging a growth mindset versus a fixed mindset.**

Positive Emotions

"If you are positive, you'll see opportunities instead of obstacles."
— *Widad Akrawi*

Barbara Fredrickson is a leading researcher in the field of positive emotions. Her book *Positivity* tells us that positive emotions broaden and build. That means they allow us to be better problem solvers and more collaborative, receptive, creative, and hopeful.

Positive emotions release the good chemical in our brains called dopamine, which provides us with feelings of pleasure, satisfaction, and motivation. It helps with memory, mood, sleep, learning, concentration, movement, and other body functions. It replaces negativity and its inevitable outcomes with good ones. Positive effects are disproportionately beneficial in their outcomes, meaning the good moments generated by positivity propel our youth upward and outward, and they mitigate the downward and inward effects of negativity.

When considering the variety of challenges some of our young people face, discussing positive emotions may seem trite. However, even in difficult situations, positive emotions such as gratitude and awe can assist us, as evident in Fredrickson's research. Prioritizing positive emotions does not suggest individuals should be happy all the time. That is not realistic for any of us. This section on positive emotions simply demonstrates the benefits that positive emotions provide. Emotions are explored further in Chapter 5, where we examine emotional management and the role negative emotions play in our lives.

> How we perceive the world around us often determines our quality of life.

Follow Jack and Rena as they demonstrate the impact of positive emotions for us. Jack and Rena enter their ninth-grade classroom to take their history exam, an exam that is important to each of them for different reasons. Jack needs good grades to secure a place on the basketball team. He has been studying for the test, is committed to doing his best, and feels pretty good about it. Rena is already planning which university she hopes to attend and is acutely aware of their strict entry criteria. Rena has also been studying extra hours and feels she knows the material well, yet she is stressed and anxious on the day of the test.

Early on, Jack encounters a difficult question he wasn't prepared for. He thinks it through, considers responses, and makes his best choice. Though Jack may have chosen incorrectly, he moves on with confidence.

When Rena encounters a similar obstacle, she panics, focusing on the fact that she had not prepared for this question. She grows increasingly anxious, moves past the question, and is now distracted, no longer functioning at her best for the remainder of the exam.

Jack addressed his challenge with positive emotions, and Rena with negative ones. Why does this matter, and how do you think the two of them will fare on the exam? What about after the exam?

How we perceive the world around us often determines our quality of life. Occasionally, hopeful and optimistic individuals can be perceived as naive or lacking understanding of the gravity or severity of situations. In actuality, often, those individuals grasp the magnitude better than most. They simply understand that achieving the best possible results requires a strategy of hope and positivity. Granted, like most things, one can take positive emotions too far and fall into naivete or frivolity, but, as a general rule, positive emotions are a strong tactic for achieving desired outcomes.

It is beneficial to have an extensive vocabulary when describing emotions. When we can be specific about what we are feeling, we can gain a better understanding of its source and impact. Positive emotions encompass more than just happiness or surprise; they also include awe, joy, excitement, contentment, pride, humility, amusement, and gratitude, among others. They are the ones that feel good. Imagine a young person who is experiencing amusement. What does their face look like? Their body language? When you are around a young person experiencing positive emotions, you can feel the energy and the receptiveness.

There are benefits to prioritizing positivity, as it:

- widens the span of possibilities, allowing you to be open to more options and consider what may have otherwise been overlooked.
- feels good, which is a worthy pursuit in itself.
- awakens the motivation to change.
- increases adaptability to frequently changing landscapes.
- transforms the future through both possibility and the views we hold.
- compounds over time, as positivity begets positivity.
- builds resources of self by assisting the development of other beneficial traits and skills.

POSITIVE EMOTION VOCABULARY

HAPPY

- **Playful**
  - Amused
  - Cheeky
- **Content**
  - Free
  - Joyful
- **Proud**
  - Successful
  - Confident
- **Accepted**
  - Respected
  - Valued
- **Powerful**
  - Courageous
  - Self-reliant
- **Peaceful**
  - Loving
  - Thankful
- **Trustful**
  - Sensitive
  - Intimate
- **Optimistic**
  - Hopeful
  - Inspired

SURPRISE

- **Startled**
  - Shocked
  - Dismayed
- **Confused**
  - Disillusioned
  - Perplexed
- **Amazed**
  - Astonished
  - Awed
- **Excited**
  - Eager
  - Energized

INTERESTED

- **Sensitive**
  - Responsive
  - Receptive
- **Allured**
  - Enticed
  - Drawn
- **Creative**
  - Engaged
  - Inspired
- **Curious**
  - Thoughtful
  - Inquisitive

Here are some tactics we use with youth to help them leverage positive emotions.

- Whenever possible, we start conversations by leading with the positive. A tale of something good that happened at school can be teased out to precede the bad event they need to discuss. No matter how tough the situation is, youth can generally find something positive. The negativity that needs to be addressed will be, and possibly more effectively. Beginning with a positive state can help youth become better problem solvers and equip them to address the issues at hand.

- When young people are ruminating on something negative, we encourage them to be intentional about where they invest their thoughts. A simple reminder is that since they choose their thoughts, they should avoid those that do not serve them and entertain those that often lead to solving the problem.

- To help youth increase awareness and perspective, when they approach us with a problem, we listen for assumptions in the story. When it sounds like they are drawing conclusions and may not have all the facts, we encourage them to reframe their thoughts by considering various interpretations of situations and not assuming their first beliefs are correct.

- The ROCK promotes positive emotions and environments by insisting on kindness in all situations. Kindness is a positive emotion that inspires more positive emotions and is explored in depth in Chapter 7. Where unkind behaviors exist among youth, or adults for that matter, positivity will struggle to prevail.

- Often, we help youth increase positive emotions by having

them call out one thing they are grateful for as they enter the program. Individuals are more likely to feel good when they reflect on the aspects of their lives that bring them benefit.

- We encourage our youth to use their character strengths, discussed in Chapter 2, to live their values, which are core to who they are as humans.
- The ROCK and Discover You™ programs provide daily opportunities for youth to connect with their peers and caring adults, building community and fostering positive emotions.
- You will find ROCK staff and students enjoying and exploring nature whenever possible. Positive emotions tend to grow just from being in the natural world.

Positive emotions can be encouraged, and when leveraged, help young people better face challenges and achieve greater success. They also make the journey of life a little better. Though positive emotions are beneficial, as mentioned earlier, one ought not expect to always feel positive. Avoid the unrealistic approach that all emotions should be positive and that we must be happy every day and in every circumstance.

Shifting our mindset doesn't happen overnight or with a single epiphany. It requires time, patience, and a series of incremental changes. Instead of trying to overhaul our way of thinking all at once, it can be more effective to concentrate on one specific situation or challenge at a time. By addressing and reflecting on smaller, manageable aspects, we can gradually build a foundation for broader change, which is discussed further in Chapter 8. This focused approach allows for more deliberate and sustained progress, making it easier to integrate new perspectives and habits into our daily lives. Each small success can serve as a stepping stone toward a more comprehensive transformation.

Equip · Inspire · Impact

- **Lead with the positive when having conversations with young people.**
- **Encourage young people to leverage positive emotions when managing challenging situations.**
- **Help young people identify areas where they could increase positivity and identify actions they could take to accomplish that.**

Gratitude

"When I started counting my blessings,
my whole life turned around."
— *Willie Nelson*

Gratitude can be described as appreciative. It can be felt and interpreted in a myriad of ways, making it difficult to define. Additionally, everyone experiences gratitude differently. Despite its simplicity, gratitude is deceptively complex. We often teach our children from a young age to be grateful by simply thanking others for a drink or help with their schoolwork. Unfortunately, this does not necessarily mean the children feel gratitude. They are merely acting out expressions of gratitude, as dictated by an external influence.

But why is gratitude so important? Why does it matter so much? Robert Emmons, author and researcher, says gratitude heals, energizes, and transforms lives. It begins with saying 'thank you' for a gift when you are a child and evolves into a sense of awe and connection with our lives and the world around us. Gratitude can help us appreciate and be more mindful of what is meaningful on our journeys.

Follow Christian as he learns about the importance of gratitude.

Christian's mom works hard to provide him with the latest game console or shoes, but he isn't grateful.

"Christian, I wish you would be grateful for what you have," sighed his mother, who'd just ended her waitressing shift. It is her second job in addition to her full-time job at the hospital. She's a single mom who sacrifices her basic needs so her son can have what he wants. She's hurt that Christian doesn't realize how much he has and lacks gratitude in general. Christian's lack of gratitude is wounding him and the people who care about him. As a result, he is angry and has little joy in his life. Mom is at a loss for how to help him develop a sense of gratefulness. He didn't seem to be so ungrateful when he was younger.

The narrative of gratitude provides the context for a sense of purpose. And being. And joy. And hope. When our youth can be grateful for the most challenging assignments because they are building toward their future, they can let go of the drudgery and move into hope for a better future. When young people can be grateful for the opportunity for an education, they can walk with resilience, knowing this is just a step along the way. When they are filled with gratitude, they appreciate gifts and embrace experiences that, while perhaps not initially desired, contribute to their personal growth and understanding.

Within Discover You™, we conduct a gratitude exercise with young people where they express appreciation to someone special in their lives. It is a specific task of writing a letter to one person. They are instructed to include details such as "I appreciate how you make sure I get to school every day and how you sat with me and watched movies the night my friends excluded me." Then, we ask them to share the letter with the recipient. Generally, at least one youth volunteers to call their person and read it to them in front of the class.

There is so much vulnerability in that action. You can expect tears of joy and complex emotions on both sides, which often provide a life-changing moment of awareness. The exhausted parent realizes their efforts have made a difference and is inspired to continue. The young person realizes they have taken an important person for granted or just haven't expressed their gratitude enough. This one gesture solidifies, heals, builds, and enhances relationships. Simply sharing gratitude with others creates awareness of a world that is intertwined, interdependent, and fragile.

Christian had an opportunity during school that week to participate in one of these exercises. He began by staring at a blank page. What did he have to be grateful for? He looked around the class, only seeing students who he felt had much more to be grateful for than he did. Still sitting with an empty piece of paper, he listened as other students began to read what they had written. Then Sheila called her mother in front of everyone.

> Gratitude is a lens through which youth can choose to see the world.

"Hi, Mom, you are on speakerphone, and my whole class is listening. We just did a thing where we wrote a letter to someone we are grateful for. I wrote about you, and I want to share it with you," declared Sheila with a slight tremor in her voice.

"Mom, I am thankful for how hard you work and how much you sacrifice for Janey and me. I am grateful that you make every Friday night movie and popcorn night. I appreciate that no matter how tired you are, you make sure we get to school and our laundry is done. I am grateful for your help with science projects."

Christian's initial thoughts were that, of course, Sheila would call her mom. They have everything, and she has so much to be grateful for. As Christian looked at Sheila now, he realized her clothes and shoes weren't brand names, and she seemed a lot like him. What she was grateful for wasn't a vacation to the ocean but a simple movie night. Christian began crafting his letter to his mom with a different tone than he had earlier in the week. That evening, he shared it with his mom, who felt a mix of awe, validation, and relief, and they experienced a positive shift in their relationship.

To increase gratitude, one can begin by reflecting on what they are grateful for and expressing it. A moment of thankfulness and reflection can alter the trajectory of one's life. Provide space for young people to observe things that deserve their gratitude, as they are everywhere. For some individuals, expressing their gratitude out loud and sharing it with others magnifies the experience. For others, it is sufficient to know it in their hearts.

A mindset of gratitude does not expect youth to be grateful for everything. Bad things and disappointments happen in everyone's lives, and it would be unwise to think that youth would or should be grateful for these situations. They can, though, seek and find gratitude daily and even pursue gratitude for small things.

Gratitude is a lens through which youth can choose to see the world. Through that lens, the world becomes a kinder, more meaningful place.

Equip · Inspire · Impact

- **Keep a gratitude journal and capture three things you are grateful for daily.**
- **Share your gratitude with someone who has played a significant role in your life.**
- **Provide space for the young people in your life to experience and express gratitude in a meaningful way.**

Thought Reframing

*"The difference between an adventure
and an ordeal is attitude."*

— *Bob Bitchin*

Thought reframing is a skill taught in cognitive behavioral therapy. It's the process of replacing negative thoughts that lack benefit and may cause harm with more helpful thoughts.

Self-talk is normal, and everyone does it. Your own voice in your head is the voice you hear the most. Often, we are our own worst enemy. You are the expert in your own life. We believe the stories we tell ourselves, so if you speak negatively about yourself to yourself or others, you begin to believe you must be right. We undermine our goals and dreams and miss opportunities. It is the internal narrative you tell yourself. It can be conscious or unconscious, spoken aloud or in our thoughts, and is incredibly powerful. Self-talk can be as simple as providing oneself with directions and can be a helpful tool for processing information. Often, we ruminate on our thoughts, that is, go over and over and over them like a broken record. Good or bad, we can repeatedly tell ourselves the same story.

Negative self-talk can be detrimental or hurtful, add to mental health challenges, or reduce self-esteem. According to the

American Psychological Association, negative self-talk is a means to substantiate negative beliefs and attitudes. Too many young people are guilty of engaging in negative self-talk, often ruminating on past mistakes and reliving negative experiences. Negative self-talk can cause us to self-sabotage. Young people can believe the message that they are undeserving or incapable, which can undermine the work they are doing to improve their lives.

Positive self-talk, on the other hand, is empowering and an act of kindness to ourselves. We can encourage and motivate ourselves to (re)build our confidence and improve our attitudes. The narrative we tell ourselves can be uplifting and even improve our performance and outcomes.

For an example of self-talk, let's examine a simple scenario with a student-athlete named Joseph. Joseph is respected by his peers, is active in the student council, earns good grades, and participates in whatever sport is in season. He appears confident and sure of himself. The truth is that Joseph is plagued with negative self-talk. He ruminates over every missed shot in basketball, whether he chooses the correct words when he speaks up in class, or if he wears the right shirt, continually repeating messages of negativity. Joseph tells himself he is a failure and stupid, and that other people think he's an idiot.

This negative self-talk wears Joseph down and, despite all his achievements, causes him to doubt himself seriously. He never feels like he is doing enough or is good enough, which hinders him from truly enjoying any activities he participates in. Logically, he knows his self-doubt is unfounded, but he can't seem to shake these thoughts. Joseph would benefit from understanding self-talk and learning the process of thought reframing, which is a straightforward approach to teaching our youth to harness their thoughts.

The ROCK employs a straightforward process to help youth

reframe their thoughts. When a young person is demonstrating negative thoughts, the following steps are used: **Notice**, **Challenge**, **Replace**, and **Repeat**.

Notice: Prompt the young person to quickly take notice of that negative thought when it enters their mind.

Challenge: Encourage the young person to challenge those thoughts. Ask themselves: Are they helpful? Where did they come from?

Replace: Direct the youth to reframe their negative thought to a positive thought that better serves them.

Repeat: Negative thoughts may pop up every few minutes, so restart the process as soon as they are noticed. Over time, the negative thoughts may become less frequent; at least the act of replacing them with positive thoughts will become a habit.

An example of thought reframing is when Joseph gets a lower grade than expected on his literature assignment. His initial thought is "You are so stupid; you'll never make it to college." After noticing it, he challenges it with "I study hard and do well in school." Finally, he replaces it with "This assignment was difficult for me, but I gave it my best. It's okay not to ace everything, especially since I generally get good grades." Joseph, feeling better about himself because he successfully halted the negative self-talk, is more likely to develop a plan to do better in the future.

This same cycle of noticing, challenging, and replacing is a tool we can share with our youth. When you hear them demonstrating negative self-talk in your presence, explain to them that what they just said is negative self-talk. Help them see that their negative language doesn't benefit them. Next, walk them through the four steps to help them shift from negative to positive self-talk. Finally, challenge them to begin noticing instances of their negative self-talk independently.

Another thought reframing application is "Have to. Want to." This version works nicely as a self-motivation tool. How often do we hear young people say they "have to" do something? They express a feeling of having to take action, such as attending a class they don't prefer. They are being forced to do something they don't want to. "Have to" is external motivation, meaning an outside force is making them do something.

> The simple act of reframing our thoughts is empowering and motivating.

"Want to" is tied to intrinsic motivation, meaning the drive comes from within. Human nature dictates intrinsic motivation as the strongest of the two. As such, we all prefer choosing over being forced. Motivation is explored further in Chapter 8.

By flipping the narrative, the action can become more palatable. Often, the story we tell ourselves is "have to" when it is actually a personal choice. For example, we tell ourselves that we "have to" go to work. In actuality, it's a choice. There may be negative consequences if we don't go to work, but that doesn't take away from the fact that it's still a choice. Even if our youth can't find a short-term "want to" for an action, they can likely add a "want to" slant if they look into their future. For example, instead of saying "I 'have to' get up early to sit through boring classes," they can say, "I 'choose to' go to school because I'm going to be an electrician. What I learn now and the grades I get will help me get a job in the future." Another example is instead of "I 'have to' eat healthy food while my friends eat anything they want," reframe it as, "I 'want to' eat healthy food because it makes me feel better, and I can maintain my health."

The simple act of reframing our thoughts is empowering

and motivating. We know if a young person doesn't want to do something, they don't have to and will find a way to circumvent whatever it is. When you overhear a young person using "have to" language, encourage them to reframe it as "want to" words. This potentially can help increase positive emotions, gratitude, hope, and autonomy.

As adults, we must remember to model this behavior by being aware of the messages we send to the youth around us. The more consistent you are with thoughts and words that are framed in a positive manner, the sooner youth will follow.

Equip · Inspire · Impact

- **Identify negative thoughts you ruminate on and how you might replace them with thoughts that better help you reach your goals.**
- **Encourage youth to Notice, Challenge, and Replace negative self-talk.**
- **Challenge youth to reframe thoughts of "Have to" to "Want to."**

Chapter 2

Strength

"Look well into yourself; there is a source of strength which will always spring up if you will always look there."
— *Marcus Aurelius*

Strength has been universally admired throughout time and across different cultures as a positive or valuable attribute. The way strength is exhibited and applied may change, but strength will always be celebrated and highly valued. That is because strength is a component of thriving, a timeless trait that allows species to survive and our world to advance. We celebrate strength in sports, arts, academics, and competitions. Yet, far too often, as a society, we focus on what we are lacking and areas that are deficits instead of strengths. This can stem from a desire to excel in or possess everything, causing us to overlook what we already have.

Picture a world where all of humanity leads with strengths. The passionate musician is celebrated with success in the arts, the agile athlete excels in sports, and the gifted writer contributes to the world through literature. Instead, we seem to spend 80% of our time focusing on our weaknesses and 20% on our strengths. We often encourage our youth to rush through what they excel at and then spend hours on areas of struggle. Flip the narrative. What if young people spent 80% of their time developing and employing their strengths and 20% of their time addressing their weaknesses?

Leading with strengths does not negate the need to seek balance and be well-rounded individuals; rather, it complements this goal. It enables people to be the best version of themselves, become more resilient, and gain the confidence to grow in areas that may require development. Witness how the 80-20 rule affects Mason and what it might look like if the narrative were switched.

> Strength is a component of thriving, a timeless trait that allows species to survive and our world to advance.

Mason excels in technology. Most of his free time is spent writing code, learning computer languages, or developing games. His tech teachers recognize his potential as significant. They encourage his parents to provide him with every opportunity to excel at this craft, as he is likely to have a solid future in technology. Mason struggles in band class, and his band teacher wants him to spend more time on music.

Who is right, and what should his parents do?

There isn't a right or wrong answer, but one of balance and realization. Yes, our youth need to be well-rounded and work hard in all areas of study. One thing they don't need is to feel like failures because they struggle in a particular area. This is why some version of the 80-20 rule applies by assigning reasonable efforts in both places. This is also why celebrating strengths is critical, supported by an acknowledgment that no one is good at everything. Mason could be encouraged to pursue his affinity for technology while setting realistic expectations for developing competence in band within the educational system. After all, he will still need a passing grade in band and all his classes, or it may negatively impact his future outlook in technology.

A key component of our work at The ROCK is developing strong youth—strong in mind, body, spirit, convictions, and beliefs—who will stand up for themselves and others, take healthy risks, and solve problems. Strength must be balanced with compassion and confidence, responsible decision-making that serves the world, and kindness.

The goal is to build a generation that surpasses our current abilities, and that requires strength on the part of the adults in the youth's lives and from the youth themselves. As a caring adult, we must put special emphasis on youth's strengths from the beginning. In the following sections, we share the ways we've cultivated strength in our youth through Discover You™.

Equip · Inspire · Impact

- **Ask a young person to share their strengths with you.**
- **Encourage a young person to visualize a future where they are leading with their strengths.**
- **Challenge a young person to focus on strengths more than deficits.**

Identifying and Ranking
Character Strengths

"Know your strengths and take advantage of them."
— *Greg Norman*

Character strengths are the positive traits of human beings as identified by Martin Seligman and Christopher Peterson, both psychologists and leaders in the field of positive psychology. Character strengths focus on what is constructive and strong about us. A strengths focus is a foundational component of positive psychology and wellbeing. The following graph illustrates the 24 character strengths, accompanied by a brief description of each. The strengths are categorized under six virtues: courage, humanity, wisdom, justice, transcendence, and temperance.

Every person possesses all 24 strengths, with each of us demonstrating a different level and combination of strengths. By knowing our youth's strengths and leveraging them, we can better support them in achieving the types of success they strive for. Some benefits of a strength-based approach for youth include increasing happiness and a sense of fulfillment, promoting better psychological health, helping them have beneficial relationships, increasing academic adjustment and success, boosting resilience

VALUES IN ACTION
24 CHARACTER STRENGTHS

COURAGE

- **Bravery**
  - Courage
  - Valor
- **Perseverance**
  - Persistence
  - Resilience
- **Honesty**
  - Truth
  - Candor
- **Zest**
  - Enthusiasm
  - Energy

JUSTICE

- **Fairness**
  - Justice
  - Impartial
- **Leadership**
  - Encouraging
  - Visionary
- **Teamwork**
  - Collaboration
  - Cooperation

TEMPERANCE

- **Forgiveness**
  - Grace
  - Pardon
- **Humility**
  - Modest
  - Without arrogance
- **Prudence**
  - Careful
  - Calculated
- **Self-Regulation**
  - Disciplined
  - Self-control

HUMANITY

- **Kindness**
  - Compassion
  - Good-Hearted
- **Love**
  - Devotion
  - Cherish
- **Social Intelligence**
  - Aware
  - Savvy

TRANSCENDENCE

- **Appreciation of Beauty & Excellence**
  - Splendor
  - Awe
- **Gratitude**
  - Appreciative
  - Thankful
- **Hope**
  - Future-focused
  - Optimistic
- **Humor**
  - Levity
  - Cheer
- **Spirituality**
  - Connection
  - Meaning

WISDOM

- **Creativity**
  - Imagination
  - Ingenuity
- **Curiosity**
  - Interest
  - Wonder
- **Judgment**
  - Discernment
  - Insight
- **Love of Learning**
  - Passion for knowledge
  - Inquisitive
- **Perspective**
  - Astute
  - Critical thinker

and problem-solving skills, and increasing engagement in their own lives. Simply put, when a strength-based approach is leveraged, it helps youth be the best version of themselves.

Here is a scenario that demonstrates how focusing on our strengths can make reaching our goals easier and even more enjoyable. Caleb approached his favorite OST staff: "Hey Matt, got a minute?"

"Sure, Caleb, what's up?" replied Matt.

"This is kind of personal, but I really want to be more active. I just don't like sports and exercise. I don't know what to do. I've been trying to force myself to work out, and it's not working," Caleb sighed. "I want to give up."

"Well, let's think about this. Trying to force myself never works for me either," said Matt. "What are some things you like to do?"

"I like my music," Caleb responded.

"Yes!" exclaimed Matt. "And you have some great moves when you are playing your music. That's exercise."

"No, that's fun," exclaimed Caleb.

"You can use what's fun for you to help you achieve your goal. Exercise isn't a one-size-fits-all," declared Matt.

Together, Caleb and Matt created a plan that provides Caleb the exercise he wants and makes him more active while leveraging his character strengths of creativity and zest. Caleb is lower on prudence and self-regulation, making it daunting to schedule activities and stick to a routine. A regimented approach frustrates him and causes him to feel as if he's failing, but by using his signature strengths, he can meet his goals while feeling good about himself. Had Caleb chosen to continue to focus on meeting his goals using tactics that didn't align with his strengths, he would have had a different experience. By focusing on his strengths, he becomes far more likely to stick to his plan and achieve the outcomes he hopes for.

The VIA Institute on Character offers a free character strengths survey on its website, and over 28 million people in 195 different countries have participated in this scientifically validated survey tool. There is an adult survey and a youth survey, which is suggested for ages 8-17. Once you complete the survey, the results can be downloaded. The free survey provides a ranking of 1-24. If youth are curious and seek more information, additional reports can be purchased that provide numerical assignments and additional details.

> When a strength-based approach is leveraged, it helps youth be the best version of themselves.

Each individual's strength profile is unique, as there are more possible combinations of strengths than people. Additionally, everyone expresses their strengths differently, making the presentation of strengths distinctly their own.

The 24 strengths are classified as signature, middle, or lesser strengths. The signature strengths, generally the top 5-7, are our superpowers. Those are most central to who the young person is and best capture their uniqueness or essence. Signature strengths reflect how they behave and are the ones that come easily to youth. They are naturally exercised, considered innate, and are the most often used strengths in their profile.

The middle strengths are those strengths generally numbered 6-17 on the survey. Middle strengths may require a bit more effort to utilize or flex than their signature strengths, as they don't feel as natural or automatic. They are character strengths that likely support or readily enhance the display of their signature strengths.

Lesser strengths are the character strengths that emerge in the bottom 4-7 of a youth's profile. These are not viewed as weaknesses but rather as strengths that are underdeveloped, unrealized, not as valued as the other strengths, or used less compared to other strengths in the profile. Lesser strengths require more energy and intentionality to put into action.

Liken the employment of strengths to that of using your hands. Your signature strengths are similar to your dominant hand. They are your automatic response. If you broke your dominant hand, you would still likely try to open a door or pick up a pen with it. Your middle strengths compare to your less dominant hand. They almost always assist your dominant hand, but they are often used in a supportive role. Since we only have two hands, we can compare our lesser strengths to tools we might pick up to complete a job. We know they are there; we just need to think about them more and be more intentional when we put them into action.

When reviewing a strengths ranking, a young person might say something such as "I thought I'd be higher in leadership." A strength may rank differently based on how a specific question was answered or perhaps what aspect of life was considered, such as home or school. This is because both settings and situations significantly impact how we perceive ourselves and how we present ourselves. For example, a younger sibling in a big family may struggle to find a voice at home, but they are a leader in a group of their peers at school. Another reason a strength, such as leadership, may be lower than expected is that sometimes it is the culmination of other strengths that make a young person a great leader. Their other strengths of prudence, fairness, and perspective contribute to their strong leadership qualities. Additionally, it is worth noting that strength ranking is a snapshot in time, and strengths can shift depending on many factors.

Through Discover You™, we teach adults how to help the young people in their lives explore their character strengths in a myriad of ways. Some ways we work directly with youth to explore character strengths include:

- Encourage youth to take the VIA Character Strength survey and review the results together.

- Prompt a conversation around how they use their character strengths.
- Review the youth's lesser strengths and discuss ways they may want to use or develop them.
- Discuss ways in which youth may want to pair different strengths together to achieve a desired outcome.
- Promote a strength-of-the-week and display it in the youth space. Acknowledge youth when they demonstrate it positively or reference it when playing games and doing activities.
- Instruct students to create a representation of their strengths via a poem, picture, essay, presentation, etc., and share it with the group. This activity brings strengths to conversations while causing youth to consider how they live their strengths.

Through our experience, we have found that when our young people identify and lean into their strengths, their outcomes and life satisfaction increase, creating an upward spiral of positive outcomes. Encouraging youth to understand their strengths can support them in times of struggle by helping them be confident in their strengths and leverage them to move toward success.

Equip · Inspire · Impact

- **Identify your top five strengths by taking the VIA Character Strength survey.**
- **Encourage youth to take the Youth VIA Character Strength survey and review the results together.**
- **Incorporate a strength-based language into your culture.**

Spotting and Balancing Strengths

"It's never too late to be who you might have been."
— *George Eliot*

When we address our youth through a strength-based lens, we empower them. Understanding that when a youth is being disruptive, they may be overusing a strength, such as humor or fairness, allows for a completely different conversation. Without considering strengths, a typical adult response might be to tell them to stop showing off or worrying about everyone else. A strength-based approach changes the conversation; perhaps the youth may be overusing the strengths of humor or fairness and could consider tempering them with lesser-used strengths like prudence or teamwork.

The goal is not to stifle strengths, but to guide young people in using the right strength at the right time and in the right amount. This approach allows the development of strong individuals without disruptive behaviors that can be associated with overusing strengths.

As you explore strengths and commit to a strength-based

approach, you begin to recognize them in others. For example, if one of the young person's strengths is creativity, you will notice a spark when they are drawing or writing and drudgery if they are in less creative situations.

A strength-based mindset is foundational to a young person's thriving, as strengths transcend deficits almost every time. The key is recognizing the need to lead with strengths and creating a common language around strengths. Youth find strength-based conversations empowering and are generally engaged when having them. They want to be their best selves and navigate this world effectively.

Join Marlana as she learns to spot and balance strengths in her students. "I don't know what to do with these kids," said Marlana, a five-year veteran English teacher. "William is constantly telling the other students what to do, Samone is disruptive and makes the others laugh when I'm trying to teach, David is always worried about everyone getting a turn. Ugh! And that's just the beginning," she continued.

"It sounds to me like you have a classroom of students who are using their strengths. Have you thought about leveraging that?" suggested Nicole, the history teacher who learned about character strengths through Discover You™.

"Leverage it? How can I leverage it when I can't control it, and I can't teach with it all going on?" Marlana asked.

"I think you would be happy with how well you can manage and develop your students using a strength-based approach," Nicole replied.

"Let's hear it. I need to try something different," said Marlana.

Spotting strengths in others helps build a culture of strength. The first step is to possess a strength-based lens and to be on the lookout for strengths.

You can spot strengths in youth and help them spot strengths in others by:

- becoming familiar with strengths. Talk about them and use them in conversation.
- looking for the things that light people up. Does the young person step easily into leadership roles? Are they curious and asking questions? Are they regularly expressing gratitude? What assignments do they volunteer for? Are they great team members?
- identifying areas they shy away from. Do they avoid details? Prefer to work independently? Do they struggle to let go of things?
- pointing out their strengths to them. It is one thing to recognize strengths; it is another to share what you've noticed. When you see a young person demonstrating a strength, call it out and name it. It doesn't need to show up as a signature strength on the survey to be impactful.

Using these steps, Marlana realized that William's strength was leadership, Samone's was humor, and David's was fairness. With this information, she was able to connect character strengths to behaviors, which led to productive conversations with each student. Marlana can name the strength and its benefits, discuss how it is being overused, and suggest using other strengths to balance out how the strength is currently manifesting itself, without sending the message to the youth that their strengths (which are a significant part of them) are negative.

Like Marlana and Nicole, you can build a strength-based culture when you encourage the youth you serve to set up goals based on their strengths, identify a new way to express a specific strength each day, refer to strengths when providing feedback both individually and collectively, engage strengths for problem-solving, and connect character strengths to behaviors.

Strength balancing, a component of a thriving strength-based culture, involves selecting the appropriate strength for the situation while ensuring it is applied at an optimal level. For example, Marlana, the overwhelmed teacher, could ask Samone, the class clown, to organize and host a talent show. With this opportunity, Samone will have a creative outlet to apply her humor in copious amounts, leading to a successful outcome in an appropriate circumstance. This method could lessen, if not eliminate, the excessive use of humor in class that is often unfavorable. When Samone is being disruptive, Marlana can also remind her that she may be overusing humor or that this isn't the best time for it.

> The goal is not to stifle strengths, but to guide young people in using the right strength at the right time and in the right amount.

There can be some key challenges for youth when working with their signature strengths. One is that they are generally unaware of their strengths, as it can be hard for them to see their strengths within themselves. Sometimes, young people view their strengths as ordinary rather than extraordinary, believing that everyone possesses the same strengths. We can all relate to this feeling; what comes naturally is easy to take for granted.

When young people put their strengths forward too strongly in a particular situation, it can be overwhelming for those around them, especially the adults in charge. For example, too much humor can present as rude, excessive curiosity can appear nosy, and strong leadership can be viewed as bossy or controlling. The child who loves to learn might start many new things without completing any of them. And the one who values forgiveness may struggle with setting boundaries.

Just as strengths can be overused, they can also be underused. For example, an underused love of learning could appear as the student not being interested in trying new things. Underused leadership may manifest as not speaking up, even when they have something to contribute. Failing to value forgiveness could result in them holding onto hurts so long that they become bitter, guarded, and affected in their mindset and self-care.

Once overused and underused strengths are spotted, we can begin teaching young people how to utilize their strengths to balance each other. Love of learning can be paired with self-regulation to help limit the specific thing they want to learn. Leadership can be paired with social intelligence to help them better understand the needs of people, or linked with perseverance to honor commitments. Forgiveness can be paired with social intelligence to recognize when others are hurting, honesty to set boundaries, judgment to help determine what is appropriate for them, or love and kindness to extend forgiveness for themselves.

Strengths are great, right? But too much of anything is, well… too much. You have a tremendous tool in hand when you are in a leadership position in a strength-based environment. Strength language leads to powerful conversations that develop and build. What do we typically do to a young person who is overusing a strength, such as leadership? When this strength manifests itself as being bossy, we tell them to stop and that their behavior is wrong. But we need strong leaders. In our attempts to "manage" behaviors, we often turn the strengths into negatives and discourage using them. That is counterintuitive to fostering resilient and strong youth.

Once you and the youth you serve understand strengths, reframe your approach. You can say, "I know how committed you are to the success of this play. However, in this situation, you may be exercising a little bit more leadership than this group needs right now. Let's amp up your fairness and humility strengths to reach a better outcome." With this statement, or one similar, you empower young people to develop and channel their superpowers in a healthy manner. It all starts with spotting their strengths and using yours.

You can spot and balance strengths when you:

- notice the behaviors and attitudes when strengths are being used.
- celebrate when you witness others using their strengths.
- take notice when you and the youth around you may be overusing a strength, and when possible, have a conversation on balancing strengths.

Remember, diversity in strengths is an asset. It's good that we are not the same. Every youth has a unique mixture of strengths that makes them individuals with their own purpose and passions. As adults who impact youth, we have an opportunity to help them develop their strengths.

Equip · Inspire · Impact

- **Identify and acknowledge strengths in others.**
- **Engage in a strength-based language when addressing challenging behaviors.**
- **Help young people identify when they may be overusing a strength and how to balance it using other strengths.**

Personal Strengths and Assets

"Start where you are. Use what you have. Do what you can."

— *Arthur Ashe*

Personal strengths are commonly considered a combination of talent, knowledge, and skills. Discover You™ includes resources and experiences as personal strengths, as both contribute to positive results. Individuals can be their best selves when they leverage their unique combinations of personal strengths. Young people can learn to recognize their own strengths and those of others and confidently operate at their highest capacity.

We begin our discussion on personal strength by examining **knowledge, skill,** and **talent**. Each person possesses a unique combination of knowledge, skills, and talents that is an integral part of their personality. Specifically, talent is innate, as it is something one is born with; skills are developed, and knowledge is gained.

Knowledge is what young people know. It is the information contained in their minds. Knowledge encompasses facts, truths, and principles acquired through studying, learning, or investigating. It includes things such as the names of the

50 states and their capitals, how a combustion engine works, and what is in our universe. Knowledge can be found on the internet, in books, magazines, podcasts, and from scholars and mentors, among other sources.

Skills are when our young people put effort into improving their ability to complete tasks. They utilize experience to perform tasks more effectively and develop skills through learning and practice. Skills may include hitting a ball with a bat, being a good writer or speaker, riding a bike, playing video games, or using a computer. These are all things that young people can improve with effort.

Talents are innate abilities with which young people are born. They are things they can do without learning or practicing. Things they do naturally that others must learn. Examples of talents include being naturally athletic, artistic, or musical. Innate talents are those with which we are naturally gifted.

Consider Charlotte and Elijah. Charlotte has always loved music. She has a knack for it, spends time pursuing information about it, and practices daily. Elijah was born with musical talent; it comes naturally to him, and he can quickly pick up new songs and instruments. Which one will be a more successful musician? They both have potential, and success often hinges on hard work. Thus, the answer is whoever is willing to work hard.

Experts debate which of the three personal strengths is most essential for success, and it is generally accepted that all three components play a role. The right mix seems to depend on the individual and the situation. A young person may have a talent, but if they don't utilize knowledge and skill, they may not develop that talent. Just as with Elijah's musical talent, its benefits remain limited until it is cultivated. You may possess all the knowledge in the world about something and still not benefit from it, such as knowing the mechanics of music but not understanding how to play an instrument. You can research music theory, which will provide you with essential knowledge, but you must also develop your skills through practice. If you are naturally talented in music, you might find it easier to develop the skill. Having a skill won't help you if you don't know how to use it. Reading music is a skill. However, applying that knowledge is what makes one a musician.

When youth leverage strengths such as these, they are more fulfilled, more likely to experience accomplishment, more likely to thrive, and more likely to struggle well when they need to. Regardless of the combination of knowledge, skill, and talent, the consensus is that there is no shortcut for hard work. In the famed words of high school basketball coach Tim Notke, "Hard work beats talent when talent doesn't work hard." As we support our youth, we must remember that hard work will be the path to their major outcomes.

Resources are another asset. Throughout life, young people can leverage numerous resources when considering what is accessible to them.

Some resources are:

- Financial
- People who can provide support or make connections to others
- Organizations that can provide support or make connections to others
- Basic needs such as transportation and housing

Generate a conversation with a young person specifically to help them identify available resources. Begin by directing your young person to consider the assets they possess in each of the four

> Young people can learn to recognize their own strengths and those of others and confidently operate at their highest capacity.

categories, being sure to prompt them to uncover resources they may not have considered. Next, discuss how each one serves as a valuable resource. Then, review each resource, examine its current uses, and consider potential new applications. Notably, some deficits can be strengths if you use them properly. For example, a lower income may open doors for financial aid.

Finally, **experiences** are also strengths. The more young people are exposed to the world, the stronger they will be in terms of healthy risk-taking and responsible decision-making. Experiences can include travel, employment, family responsibilities, or participation in clubs or on sports teams.

Youth can be guided to explore their different experiences and creatively consider how those experiences can be strengths. The following section looks deeper into how young people can apply skills gained in one area of life to reduce the learning curve in different situations.

Creating a strength-based language and approach may help young people understand they have more strengths and resources than they realize. This can help them take a different approach to those resources or skills they may be lacking by recognizing that they can be developed or cultivated.

Equip · Inspire · Impact

- Encourage youth to identify areas where they possess talent, knowledge, and skills.
- Direct young people to inventory their resources, including financial, personal, and professional connections, as well as organizations and basic needs.
- Assist young people in evaluating their personal strengths and experiences, including participation in clubs and travel.

Self-Efficacy

"We are what we believe we are."

— *C. S. Lewis*

Self-efficacy is a person's belief in their ability to complete a task or achieve a goal. Often, we develop a belief in ourselves or our abilities based on past experiences that are either relatable or successful. It is the idea that "I can because I have." Simply put, when you have achieved something, it directly influences your ability to believe you can accomplish something else.

Consider Dylan. Dylan struggles to make friends. He hasn't had a good friend in his 14 years, he feels awkward around peers, and his isolation is beginning to affect his mental health. The adults around him notice that he's struggling, but they are at a loss about what they can do to support him. They encouraged him to meet neighbors, volunteer, or join clubs to find friends with similar interests, but none of that has worked. He's a nice kid, funny, and a little quirky—no different than most kids his age.

Ask yourself, What is one thing that could help Dylan move forward?

Perhaps if he could just make one friend, he would realize he could do it and be able to replicate that success. In practice, this is self-efficacy, which states that one's perception of their capabilities directly influences the outcome of future events. In this case, the first step is to help Dylan identify the skills he already possesses.

Dylan had started to trust our Discover You™ staff after attending several of our weekly workshops at his school. The workshop on self-efficacy really caught Dylan's attention. One of the Discover You™ team members shared how this tool had recently helped them secure a college scholarship. Another team member mentioned how he wished he'd had this tool when he was growing up. He could have used it to make friends, as that had been difficult for him. That vulnerability inspired Dylan to privately share his struggle and ask if the process might benefit him. Our team's response? "There's only one way to find out."

Research on transferable skills suggests that knowledge gained in one area can be transferred to another area. Transferable skills are often referred to in the workforce, but our youth interactions demonstrate that they are also true for them. Youth bring a variety of experiences; some they would consider more successful than others. In every experience, they learn things, be it what to do or what not to do. It is by reflecting upon those experiences that youth learn how to transfer current skills to future experiences. With practice and awareness, knowledge in one area can be transferred to another. As youth recognize these skills, they increase their confidence and resilience. You can play an essential role in helping youth recognize skills gained in one situation and learn how to apply those same skills elsewhere.

In the graphic, you'll see the bubble prompts completed by Dylan, who wants to make friends. These prompts include identifying the goal, skills needed, similar things they've done, and things to avoid, and then creating a plan. We also include classmate Angie's responses to demonstrate how these same prompts can serve very different goals. Angie is about to start her first job and is doubting she has the skills to do so successfully.

SELF-EFFICACY PROMPTS
DYLAN

GOAL

Make a friend this school year

SKILLS I NEED

- Be friendly
- Be relatable
- Be available

SIMILAR THINGS I HAVE DONE

- Spending time with cousins
- Relating to teammates on last year's robotics team

WHAT I HAVE LEARNED

- People enjoy talking about common interests
- I like helping others

WHAT NOT TO DO

- Be pushy
- Talk only about myself
- Say no to fun activities I have time for

PLAN

- Join a new group after school
- Volunteer at local electronics club
- Join someone sitting alone at lunch

SELF-EFFICACY PROMPTS
ANGIE

GOAL

Be successful at my summer job at the grocery store

SKILLS I NEED

- Be reliable
- Be focused
- Operate a cash register

SIMILAR THINGS I HAVE DONE

- Being attentive at school
- Focusing well on homework
- Having good computer skills

WHAT I HAVE LEARNED

- I enjoy work
- I like people
- I am motivated

WHAT NOT TO DO

- Only do tasks I like
- Miss work without good reason
- Attempt a task I do not understand without help

PLAN

- Be on time for work every day
- Be nice to customers
- Ask for clarification on tasks I don't understand

Dylan and Angie have each identified their applicable skills and abilities. Now, let's associate transferring skills with self-efficacy. Albert Bandura, psychologist and originator of social cognitive theory, defined self-efficacy as people's ability to judge their capabilities and, based on those abilities, develop a plan to achieve their desired outcomes.

I can because I already have. When young people have self-efficacy, they believe they are capable of achieving goals. They believe they can translate what they learned from one situation into the ability to manage a similar situation. In this case, Dylan and Angie have demonstrated to themselves that they possess the skills they need to achieve their goals. Now, they believe they can accomplish their goal based on the knowledge that they have accomplished something similar. They can apply those same skills to move forward and achieve other things. With increased confidence, they can move forward in pursuing their respective goals.

When you have achieved something, it directly influences your ability to believe you can accomplish something else.

These are also beliefs based on reality and effort. That's important. When working with young people, we utilize real-life skills and behaviors they have developed, rather than making meaningless statements. We didn't suggest they could do the job because they were born amazing, but because they took action. Reality, not vague notions, makes the difference. This engages a growth mindset, as we explored in Chapter 1. The understanding that effort and hard work yield results extends beyond relying on natural brilliance. Effort and hard work are more sustainable and replicable than relying on fixed characteristics or having a fixed mindset. When we rely on what is fixed, we will always reach a limit, hitting a low ceiling. The potential becomes virtually limitless when we rely on what we can grow and develop.

The belief that "I can because I have" enables youth to recognize past successes, apply those wins to future opportunities, increase their self-confidence, and then create a plan, ultimately taking action and accomplishing their goals. How hard will it be for Dylan to make friends if he doesn't believe he can? Who will hire Angie if even she doesn't believe she can do the job? These prompts and conversations teach young people a valuable life lesson: that to move forward in life, they must first believe in themselves and their abilities.

Equip · Inspire · Impact

- **When youth seek to build confidence in an area, assist them in identifying times when they have experienced success in something similar.**
- **Prompt youth to work through identifying the goal, skills needed, similar things they've done, and things to avoid, and then to create a plan.**
- **Teach them the importance of a growth mindset and that they, like their talents, are always growing and evolving.**

Chapter 3

Resilience

"The oak fought the wind and was broken, the willow bent when it must and survived."

— *Robert Jordan*

Resilience is a young person's ability to bounce back. It is defined as the capacity to recover from or adjust easily to misfortune or change. To be resilient is to recover quickly from obstacles and weather the inevitable difficulties of life. It is a critical skill to be able to accept those challenges as a natural part of the process and use them as a catalyst for personal development and a deeper understanding of oneself and the world.

Resilience is a capacity or outcome that results from a combination of other skills, knowledge, and assets. These include, but are not limited to:

- Emotional awareness and regulation
- Self-efficacy
- Hope
- Growth mindset
- Flexible and accurate thinking

- Empathy
- Connection
- Impulse control
- Self-regulation
- Effective problem solving
- Sense of meaning
- Positive self-perceptions
- Valued talents
- Humor
- Character strengths

You may notice similarities between the list and the content covered in this book, which is no coincidence. The foundational skills we focus on lead to resilient youth. However, there is no single path to building resilience in our youth.

Compare resilience to a plastic straw and lack of resilience to a wooden pencil. When placed under similar adverse forces, the straw will bend with the force, quickly returning to its original and functional state when the pressure is released. The pencil, however, snaps in two. With more effort, the pencil remains functional but does not recover in the same manner as the straw.

Why are some people more resilient than others? One consideration is that there are protective or external factors that are key for youth to be resilient, including:

- families who have high cohesion and low discord, meaning they function well as a unit.
- appropriate and supportive parenting.
- other positive relationships, such as caring adults and prosocial peers.
- community that provides good neighborhoods and high-minded organizations.

In contrast, some of our most resilient youth have few of these protective factors, which I have always found fascinating. In my observation, many other contributing elements, such as living in a dysfunctional environment, may force young people to be resilient.

To illustrate, this is Rohan's story. Rohan is an incredibly resilient seventh-grade student. He rarely misses a day of school or his after-school program. When he fails at something or struggles, he recovers quickly and doesn't seem to be impacted. Yet, he has few protective factors. His home life provides him with more barriers than support. He is often left to fend for himself with meals, clean clothes, and homework. Supportive adults outside of school and after-school programs are essentially nonexistent.

But as mentioned, Rohan is incredibly resilient. According to research, genetics and biological factors can contribute to a predisposition that promotes resilience. Earlier, we examined several other factors that contribute to resilience, one of which is failing well, which we'll discuss later in the chapter. Among other things, good or bad, Rohan's situation has afforded him the opportunity to make his own choices and experience the consequences of those choices. Those skills he developed out of necessity have likely provided him with the critical skill of resilience.

Resilience is a skill that can be developed. How we address a situation or conversation can significantly impact the outcome, especially when we are fostering skills in youth, such as resilience. It is often quicker and easier for adults to find solutions and disseminate wisdom when a young person is struggling. However, it isn't our wisdom we intend to develop. It is our experience that youth learn at a deeper level and can apply concepts to their own lives more effectively when they solve the problems themselves.

While we can do our best to help build resilience in young people, we can't do the work for them. We must remember that they may not immediately change their mindset. It could take time. In that time, it might be helpful to consider that youth will solve problems when necessary, even if it's not how we would solve them. And if it doesn't go right the first time, they will likely try again. Excessive, misplaced intervention from adults can directly obstruct this natural process of failing and trying, so I caution you to consider the impact of intervening before youth have the opportunity to act independently.

The good news is that generally, the more youth fail or struggle, the better problem solvers and the more resilient they become. This becomes possible when we stop doing for them what they can do for themselves. This includes age-appropriate personal care, chores, cleaning up after themselves, setting alarms and managing their time, asking for help when needed, etc.

As mentioned throughout the book, skills are most effectively developed through doing and experiencing. For example, in ROCK programs, staff seek opportunities to engage and develop skills in participants, including working together to set up and clean up the program space and prepare items for activities.

> The more youth fail or struggle, the better problem solvers and the more resilient they become.

Duncan was a seventh-grade boy in our OST program who experienced great distress with minor setbacks. It happened when an activity was slated to begin at 4:00, and it was 4:10. It happened when the catapult he built didn't launch or when he spilled his milk. His excessive reactions, including stomping and raising his voice, served neither Duncan nor the program. Some tactics we engaged to increase Duncan's resilience included co-creating and implementing strategies before something broke down.

It was Simple Machines Week in OST, and the students, including Duncan, would be building a winch using cardboard tubes, string, straws, and a spool. The winch would be used to load a rocket onto the launch pad, both of which were pending construction. After the students referenced the supply list and gathered the necessary items from the bins, a staff member asked, "How many times was NASA successful on their first try?" That broad question opened a robust discussion. Are we talking about winches, rockets, or space travel? "Choose any component," said the staff. "How many times did they get it right on the first attempt?" The resounding answer was, "Probably never."

"How many of you will build a flawless winch on the first try?" the staff asked. With the group considering this, the staff said, "Success is not found on a direct path. It is in the willingness to fail, get back up, and try again. And again. And again." They continued, "Now, who here is ready to experiment with building a winch?"

Duncan and the other students agreed. When Duncan's winch failed, he was challenged to think like a scientist and try again. The entire experiment went as a middle school STEM project should, with youth learning resilience through being allowed to fail and struggle their way to success. As a result of this experience, Duncan began to find he could handle setbacks and rebound from them relatively quickly. Over the year, he demonstrated increased amounts of resilience and the ability to fail well.

We have seen that resilient youth are more likely to be both confident and compassionate, optimistic and flexible in their thinking, responsible and patient, effective communicators, and better at working as a team and solving problems individually and collectively. Resilience enhances self-awareness and facilitates the productive management of behaviors, thoughts, and emotions. As our youth develop resilience, these benefits will be invaluable to them throughout their lives.

Equip · Inspire · Impact

- Demonstrate to youth the importance of flexing under stress and returning to a functioning state using the aforementioned straw and pencil imagery.
- Allow youth to fail and discover solutions independently.
- Allow youth to experience age-appropriate consequences and solve problems.

Grit

"The most certain way to succeed is
always to try just one more time."
— *Thomas Edison*

Angela Duckworth, psychologist, researcher, and author, describes grit as passion and sustained persistence focused on long-term achievement. Duckworth says grit requires self-control, resilience, and ambition.

Consider Jennifer's example. Jennifer works hard, applies herself, and performs well academically. Her mother is a doctor, and her father is a lawyer. Her parents don't feel they are pushing her in any direction, as either of their professions is more than acceptable career choices for Jennifer. Jennifer is dedicated to her studies in science, pursuing a degree in medicine. This often feels daunting for Jennifer as she increasingly realizes she is not passionate about medicine. She fears that a lack of passion and commitment will make advanced education more difficult and that she may not find success.

Jennifer loves her science classes and lights up when studying the environment. She catches herself reading research on sustainable farming and clean water projects well into the night. Jennifer knows she wants to make a difference by developing sustainable solutions to provide basic resources to remote locations worldwide. Jennifer recognizes it's time to have a conversation with her parents. She believes she could probably make it through medical school relying on the persistence aspect of grit, but will likely eventually falter, as the passion isn't present for her. At the least, Jennifer may not feel fulfilled if she neglects to pursue the work she is passionate about. Grit is passion and persistence, which, when combined, yield results.

Understanding grit highlights the importance of young people discovering their passion and true calling. One can achieve a level of success without passion, but it is passion that drives and sustains it. Passion, purpose, and meaning are intertwined. IQ or intelligence isn't the only factor separating successful students from those who struggle. It is often the level of grit that is highly predictive of success.

> Grit requires self-control, resilience, and ambition.

Grit is not solely applicable to those whom society considers high achievers. Not everyone will or should be an Ivy League graduate or an Olympic competitor. Some individuals may struggle in a classroom setting, and for them, achieving a passing grade can be a significant accomplishment, which should be equally celebrated. Success is relative, and we want to ensure we do not marginalize those whose level of success doesn't match our perception of success.

Equip · Inspire · Impact

- Encourage youth to develop grit by staying engaged in commitments as long as it is logical.
- Provide youth with opportunities to pursue their passion, purpose, and meaning by allowing them to experience the world around them.
- Help young people set long-term goals to build their grit capacity. Be sure to evaluate periodically to ensure persistence and passion are intact and that the goal remains appropriate.

Stupid Grit

"New beginnings are often disguised as painful endings."
— *Lao Tzu*

There is a degree of grit known as stupid grit. Our youth need to be able to apply grit in their current circumstances, gain wins, build on wins, repeat, and do their best to avoid "stupid grit." Caroline Miller, researcher and author, coined the term stupid grit. Miller defines stupid grit as the unwillingness to discontinue the pursuit of a goal that no longer serves the individual. Miller continued with the concept of authentic grit, which includes positive outcomes and avoids stupid grit.

Stupid grit looks like someone refusing to quit because they are "not a quitter," so they remain in toxic situations and relationships or continue investing their time into something that doesn't serve them. On occasion and in extreme situations, loss of life and permanent damage can result from pursuits that should be abandoned.

An example of stupid grit in teenage relationships might be staying in a clearly unhealthy or unfulfilling relationship just for the sake of sticking it out. For instance, if a teenager is in a relationship with frequent arguing, silencing, lack of respect, or emotional manipulation and refuses to break up or address the issues because they're determined to make it work despite repeated problems, that's a form of stupid grit.

A young person might persist in staying with their partner or friend out of a sense of obligation or because they don't want to appear like they're giving up, even when it's evident that their efforts are leading to more harm than good. This kind of persistence overlooks the importance of healthy relationship dynamics and self-respect, leading to prolonged dissatisfaction and emotional strain.

> Youth need to be able to apply grit in their current circumstances, gain wins, build on wins, repeat, and do their best to avoid "stupid grit."

Take Jackson as an example of over-commitment. Jackson is involved in baseball, soccer, and track, as well as the debate team and student council, and participates in the band. He considers himself a hard worker who keeps his obligations, but his mom is concerned that he's overcommitted. "It is good to be active as long as you have balance," she nudged him.

"I'm not a quitter, Mom," replied Jackson. "Sure, there are some things I am not enjoying as much as I thought I would, but I don't want to give up."

"How about we evaluate each one together?" Mom asked.

Jackson and his mom created a list of criteria to consider for each commitment. They began by deciding how many hours per week Jackson wanted to be involved in extracurricular activities, taking into account seasons when there would be additional demands on his time, such as studying for exams or attending family events.

Here are the criteria Jackson and his mother used.

- Does it provide what you hoped for when you began?
- Is it a positive experience, engaging, and/or fun?
- Is it a good use of your time?
- Does it align with your long-term goals?
- Will your lack of participation have a significant negative impact on others' ability to participate?
- How long is the commitment? And how many hours does it require?

Jackson listed everything he was involved in, the number of hours he spent on each activity per week, and when each commitment ended. Deciding became easier when he realized he didn't want to spend more than eight hours per week combined on these activities.

His mother didn't do this for him; she did it with him. That's important to note. Once Jackson clarified his priorities, he decided to stay in one sport and one club at a time and resign from the rest. He fulfilled his current commitments as best he could, letting the leaders of each group know that he would not be returning. He felt confident when he determined it necessary to resign immediately from the student council, as the commitment was too much, and he recognized it would not significantly impact the organization.

Most of all, Jackson realized much of what he had been considering grit was stupid grit, as some of the commitments no longer served him and were acting against him. He didn't quit or give up; he made a different, informed decision. Jackson's grit served him well and will likely continue to contribute to his success throughout his life. His passionate and persistent traits, once reviewed and thoughtfully adjusted, continued to help him excel.

Equip · Inspire · Impact

- Ensure youth understand the difference between being responsible and keeping their commitments and stupid grit.
- Use the criteria Jackson and his mom used to encourage youth to evaluate their commitments.
- Support youth in properly ending commitments and relationships that no longer serve them.

Failing Well

"What's comin' will come, an' we'll meet it when it does."
— *Rubeus Hagrid, Harry Potter and the Goblet of Fire*

We all struggle at some point, just as we will all fail at some point. Even when you're proficient at something, you're still bound to experience occasional failure. To truly be competent in most things, we should not only anticipate failure but also set goals that include an expectation of failing frequently along the way.

But how do you react to that failure? It's okay to get frustrated. It's okay to cry. But then what? What's your next step? Being able to analyze the situation and extract lessons from failure is an example of failing well. It means handling failure in a way that promotes growth, learning, and resilience. It's about turning setbacks into valuable experiences and maintaining a constructive approach to mistakes or disappointments. Avoid equating the failure with being a failure or a sign that the task just isn't for you.

Failure is often subjective. One student might view a C as a failure, while another might see that same C as a success. Either way, the path to success is riddled with failure. Let's say you were able to build a high-functioning engine on the first try without any mistakes or failures. The probability of creating the highest-functioning engine increases exponentially with the number of failures identified through trials and testing. The failed tests would reveal opportunities for improvement in distance and other performance metrics. Without knowing what doesn't work, you have not tried everything that might work.

> One of the greatest skills we can teach young people is to fail well. And to fail often.

As adults, we must be particularly mindful of how we both directly and indirectly define and react to failure, whether our own or that of others. I'll use the example of Coach Hendrick, a likable high school coach with high expectations for his athletes. There's a poster in his office of an Olympic skier with the words "Failure is not an option" written across the top. Coach Hendrick has invited Mr. McKay into his office to inform him that his son, Arthur, is on the verge of getting cut from the basketball team.

"I know it means a lot to him, and he could probably do it. He gets nervous and makes uncharacteristic mistakes," shared Coach Hendrick.

Mr. McKay is well aware of his son Arthur's struggles on the team and believes that part of those struggles comes from Coach Hendrick.

"We encourage students to put themselves out there. I don't know what the problem is," said Coach Hendrick.

"Arthur is afraid of failing," replied Mr. McKay, "and it negatively affects his game. He used to love basketball, but now he dreads it."

"Well, he doesn't get that from here. Here, we teach practice and hard work, and you can make mistakes," replied Coach Hendrick.

"Do you? Perhaps we can discuss the messages you are sending to the kids?" asked Mr. McKay as he looked at the poster.

What messages do we send to our youth? Are you sending a

consistent message that failure is not only tolerable but also fun and critical to growth and learning? Or have the constraints of grades and performance put people in a position of feeling that failure is acceptable only under certain circumstances? Perhaps you can fail in a game but not on a test?

One of the greatest skills we can teach young people is to fail well. And to fail often. Encouraging failure seems a bit counterintuitive, doesn't it? We want to protect our young people, don't we? Give them everything, make sure they are safe, and that their path is clear? Often, our best intentions can undermine our desired outcome. Our kids need to be able to fail and fail well. They need to anticipate failure and celebrate it.

Failing well is directly related to a growth mindset, which we explored in Chapter 1. The ability to fail well is essential for resilience. Life involves failure. When people fear failure, they may be limited in their performance and willingness to take risks, which can lead to underperformance.

"I have not failed. I've just found 10,000 ways that won't work," said Thomas Edison regarding the light bulb. One doesn't actually fail until they stop trying. However, like stupid grit, one can go too far, as there are clearly times one should abandon a quest. Using the criteria outlined in the former section helps determine whether a pursuit is worth going the extra distance for. When it is a worthy pursuit, here are some ways to support young people in failing well. It's worked for The ROCK, and it may work for you, too.

- **Normalize it**. Embrace failure as a positive experience; it's a natural part of life.
- **Manage expectations.** The expectation should not be to always succeed. Failing should be built into the plan from the beginning.
- **Remove signs and stigma.** Replace messages that suggest

failure is not an option with those that support failure as part of the process.

- **Reach high.** Remind youth that if they're never failing, they aren't reaching far enough.
- **Celebrate failures.** Encourage youth not only to tolerate but also to celebrate their failures. Failing is a form of growth, and growth should be applauded.
- **Learn from failure.** Use failing for what it is: a learning opportunity. The path to success is riddled with failures.
- **Failure is an event.** Define failure as something that happened, not a label on a person. A person who experiences failure is not a failure.

Our youth, in a literal, not theoretical sense, possess the solutions to the known problems of today and the looming problems of tomorrow. The solutions will likely be complex, and this generation must not only be willing to fail but to embrace failure. Doing something that hasn't been done before requires risk and creativity. Their path to solutions will include failures, but it is through these failures that they will find the solutions.

Here are some conversation starters we've used to talk about failing that you can use to generate dialogue with the young people in your life.

- How do you define success?
- How do you define failure?
- What are you worried will happen if you fail?
- How many failures are between you and your dreams?
- How many times will you need to, or are willing to, fail to reach your dreams?
- What failures are inevitable in achieving your dreams?
- What are you willing to risk to achieve your goals?
- What are you waiting for?

- What happens if you're successful?
- What do you learn from failure?

It's also important to share your stories of failure because, by being accessible, your experiences are more relatable. Sharing your failures demystifies failure and proves that it's a normal part of life. Popular role models are also helpful; you could encourage students to read a book about Michael Jordan or other individuals who have achieved success despite adversity and failure. Remember the growth mindset we discussed in Chapter 1? Sharing your failures with young people also promotes a growth mindset, demonstrating the value of using failures as lessons. It additionally models vulnerability, which increases trust and open communication. In our effort to help young people fail well, we must also be vulnerable and share our own struggles.

Equip · Inspire · Impact

- **Evaluate the messages you send regarding failure.**
- **Normalize failure as part of learning and achieving goals.**
- **Set high expectations that factor in and support failure.**

Learning Loop

*"Life is divided into three terms: that which
was, which is, and which will be. Let us learn
from the past to profit by the present, and from
the present, to live better in the future."*

— *William Wordsworth*

The Learning Loop is a simple evaluation tool with broad
applications, designed by researchers Michelle McQuaid and Peggy
Kerns. It gauges performance and learning objectives and can be
used for self-assessment, in one-on-one scenarios, or in groups.
Essentially, a Learning Loop looks like this:

- An action took place.
- Evaluate that action using the following prompts:
  - What went well?
  - How did you struggle? What were your challenges?
  - What will you do differently the next time?

The Learning Loop has been one of the most valuable tools for
me in my role as leader of The ROCK. The first time I realized the
Learning Loop was something I would need to leverage was inside
a police car.

Growing up a tad bit rebellious and extremely adventurous, I often wondered what my first ride in a police car would be like. Would it be a case of mistaken identity, being in the wrong place at the wrong time, or of unpaid parking tickets? Obviously, I wasn't as rebellious as I thought. My answer came at about 1 a.m. on a Saturday morning in September, following a seven-hour shift with a few hundred teens at our Friday night event.

That year, I participated in a local leadership program, which, among other commitments, provided each participant with the opportunity to explore our community. Due to the nature of the work I did, I opted to do a ride-along with a local police officer. On my assigned evening, I jumped into Officer Paul's cruiser to head out on patrol. To my inner teenager's surprise, I was in the front seat, and provided I kept it together, this ride would continue to be a voluntary one.

> The goal is to help young people develop to their highest level of functioning.

We patrolled county roads not far from the teen center. Most of the time, we chatted about the challenges youth faced and shared stories of our adventures. The patrol mainly involved driving around in the dark, with Officer Paul occasionally running the plates of the rare cars we encountered. Not many people were on the roads in that part of Michigan at that time of the morning. Without warning, he activated his lights to signal the car in front of us to pull over. It seemed the driver was weighing their options as they hesitated to stop but ultimately complied without incident.

Officer Paul gave me a stern look and instructed me to stay in the vehicle. I complied. After what seemed like forever, with Officer Paul coming and going between vehicles, a young man in handcuffs was escorted to the squad car's back seat. What do you do in that situation? I had no clue. Clearly, we'd be together for a bit, as we were at least 15 minutes from where I expected this man would be going.

I turned around to say hello, thinking this was a life-altering moment for whoever was in the backseat. As I started to introduce myself, I recognized the face that greeted me. "Hey, Justin, how are you doing?" Justin had graduated from high school two years prior. He attended The ROCK in middle and high school, but was no longer eligible due to his age. I would let him and his buddies come in and play basketball in the gym when we weren't open for the younger students. I got to know him pretty well in his earlier years at The ROCK. Generally speaking, the more trouble a kid got into, the better I knew them.

He looked at me, a bit puzzled, and said, "I've had better nights. What are you doing here?"

I explained that I was participating in a ride-along with Officer Paul as part of a leadership program. "What are you doing here?" I asked while the officer arranged for a wrecker to tow Justin's vehicle.

"Expired plates. And insurance. And my license."

"Hm, well, consistency is good" was my optimistic reply. When I prodded him, he admitted that he would have no one to call to get him out if he were detained.

I exited the car to talk to the officer. "Ma'am, you really need to stay in the car," he reminded me.

"I know, I was just wondering what will happen to Justin. I know him. He attended The ROCK when he was younger and still plays basketball with us during our off hours," I replied, concerned.

He explained that he'd take Justin to jail, where he would be booked and remain until he either posted bail or appeared before the judge.

"Would it be offensive to you if I bailed him out?" As a mother, I was struggling with letting this young man spend the night in jail.

"It's your money," smiled Officer Paul.

What started as a long day and an even longer evening turned into a never-ending night. After posting bail, I drove Justin home, 20 minutes in the opposite direction of my house, and in the middle of nowhere. At about 6 o'clock in the morning, I finally arrived at my warm bed, feeling good about showing a young man I believed in him and that he had value. For the price of $150, which meant no extras like ordering lunch out for the next month, I helped turn a life around, and I looked forward to our conversations about his future. College may be an option for Justin now, I thought, drifting off.

After a few hours of sleep, I went to work, and a few of Justin's buddies rolled in. "Hey, where's Justin? How's he doing?" I asked.

"He's in jail," one replied.

Feeling more informed than his buddies and a bit like the cool aunt, I provided the update, "No, he was for a bit last night, but I bailed him out. He's home."

The tallest of the three said, "Yeah, well, this morning, when he got his car out of the impound lot, they busted him driving away with it."

To say I was shocked would be an understatement. Nothing had changed in the past few hours; thus, once again, Justin was driving without a valid driver's license, license plate, and vehicle insurance. And doing so after I had spent $150, which I could have really used elsewhere, to get him out of trouble. The next month of brown-bag lunches afforded me many opportunities to consider how I might have actually helped Justin, rather than merely saving him from spending a night in jail.

I went through the Learning Loop, although I didn't have a name for it at the time. This straightforward, three-step tool allows us to evaluate our actions and move forward in a positive manner: **Act. Assess. Adjust. What went well? What did you struggle with? What will you do differently next time?**

THE
LEARNING
LOOP

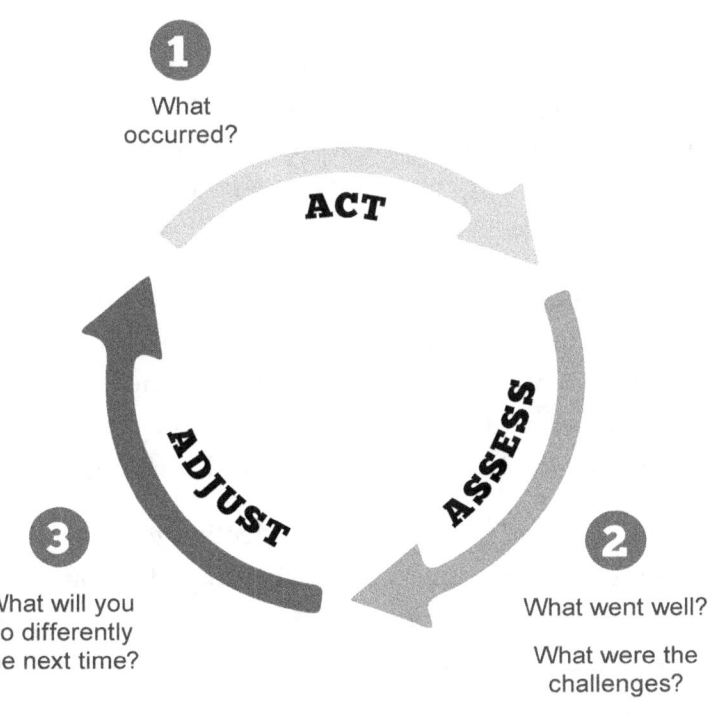

1

What
occurred?

ACT

ASSESS

ADJUST

3

What will you
do differently
the next time?

2

What went well?

What were the
challenges?

Act: In this instance, I spent my hard-earned money posting bail for a young man who had made a conscious choice in his behavior.

Assess: What went well? That took a moment. One good thing was that I was there and able to support Justin, although he seemed much more experienced in that sort of thing than I was. Officer Paul and his buddies also had comical fodder for their morning coffee. Both were pretty good wins.

The next assessment question, "What did I struggle with?" provided a range of thoughts. First, I jumped too quickly to be the hero without thinking of the consequences of my actions or how Justin might have actually been helped. I clearly struggled, as my personal sacrifice was not only not helpful but hurtful. I potentially sent the wrong message to Justin, implying he could do what he wanted without personal consequences.

Adjust: What would I do differently next time? Certainly, I would not rush to bail someone out of something when I don't understand the circumstances or the implications. This marked a turning point for me as I began to consider the distinction between equipping and enabling.

The Learning Loop is also an effective tool for youth. You can use it to ask questions and provide space for young people to find their answers. This helps develop problem-solving skills and independent thinking. You may know the answers, but restrain for a moment and let them figure it out.

What went well?
We begin by highlighting what went well to capitalize on the

outcomes of positive emotions, as discussed in Chapter 1. According to researcher Fredrickson, positivity enables us to be better problem solvers and more open to potential solutions. It prepares us to do the work that will follow.

Encourage young people by asking curious questions as needed. Once they thoughtfully respond, you can build on the successes of the youth to help them identify items they may have overlooked. You can make suggestions or ask questions such as "How well did your robot perform?" or "The design was innovative."

What did you struggle with?

Or what challenges did you encounter? When adults present this question, space is created for youth to evaluate their efforts and circumstances. Again, as the observing adult, you probably have many ideas about the struggles and challenges, but providing youth the opportunity to identify these on their own helps ensure future success and develop critical thinking skills.

Once again, you can interject supportive feedback after the youth thoughtfully responds. At this point, you can ask pointed questions to ensure they identify other areas to potentially improve upon. Providing feedback this way allows the youth to accept it without feeling criticized.

What might you do differently the next time?

Youth, especially adolescents, need to have autonomy, which is the freedom to make personal choices. Adults telling young people what they need to do is sometimes appropriate, but not beneficial in every situation. The goal is to help young people develop to their highest level of functioning. Asking this question allows the young person to consider possibilities and solutions and to explore their own thoughts and ideas.

It can be challenging to refrain from disseminating all your acquired knowledge. However, at this moment, your wisdom is in remembering that your role is to guide and coach, not to do and direct. This tactic helps our youth be self-motivated to improve. You can be confident that they gained skills and abilities as critical thinkers and problem solvers.

When youth explore what they would do differently next time, a growth mindset approach begins to form. This simple question embodies the developmental mindset discussed in Chapter 1. It is all about valuing effort, the ability to change, and a willingness to fail and try again.

The next time a young person is faced with trying circumstances or situations, activate the Learning Loop using three questions:

- What went well?
- What did you struggle with?
- What will you do differently the next time?

Equip · Inspire · Impact

- **Familiarize yourself with the Learning Loop and utilize it for personal development.**
- **Use the Learning Loop to debrief with young people when feedback is appropriate.**
- **Teach the Learning Loop to young people, encouraging them to use it independently to evaluate situations and performance.**

Part II

Courage. Confidence. Connection.

Courage. Confidence. Connection.

"You are braver than you believe, stronger than you seem, and smarter than you think."

— *A.A. Milne*

It was 10:00 on a Friday night, and parents would soon pick up their teens from the weekly Friday night gathering at the center. There were over 250 teens that week, most of whom were too young to drive. I approached the welcome desk, an area where I would find whoever was most recently caught doing something they should not have been doing. I was not surprised that one staff member and four teenage boys gathered behind it. Middle and high school students came from across our rural and suburban counties, so something always happened when that many teens were gathered in one place.

There sat Chance, who was small, even as a sixth grader. Chance was always surrounded by his JV football team, cheerleaders, and anyone else who could make the cut. He was likable, sporting a crooked grin and quick smile. And I knew him well, even though he had only been attending for a short time. Chance sat with his back to the crowd's comings and goings, with three of his friends beside him, facing the staff member, Max.

"What's up, Chance?" I casually put out there. Many years ago, I learned not to overreact and not to give the impression that something was going extremely wrong when interacting with youth.

As Chance sat on the old wooden bench, his arms folded tightly across his chest, rocking himself back and forth, his face taut with trembling lips and tears streaming down, it was evident that the situation was intense.

"I'm done. I'm going to do it. I'm going to kill that man." Chance paused and, in the most anguished voice I'd ever heard, his fists clenched and pounding his thighs, said, "I got a gun. When I'm done, I'm turning it on myself. He's not treating my mom like that anymore." Still looking me in the eyes, he said, "And you can't talk me out of it. You don't have to live there." He was right. I didn't have to live there. I could see his pain, almost feel it, yet I was only a witness to his torment.

I recognized Chance's courage in sharing his intentions with someone. He had undoubtedly suffered with these thoughts for some time, and by working up the courage to speak them out loud, I believed he was serious and asking for help.

"Hey, Chance, I hear you, and I'm not going to do that. How about you, Max, and I hang out for a bit, and we send the rest of these folks on their way?" I asked. Max was our staff member who had earned the right to have a real conversation with Chance. He was the first to greet Chance and his friends when they initially walked into the center, as confident but terrified graduating fifth-graders. Max was an expert at building relationships with youth. He interacted with all the students and was proficient at keeping the communication lines open by asking about football games, school tests, and what was important to each of them. He played basketball with them and casually intervened if things got rough with opposing groups of kids. He gained their confidence by showing up at their school for one of their football games and then hanging around to tell them "nice tackle" and "good play," even though they had lost that night.

Building relationships and trust with the youth often requires going above and beyond. It is a process that requires sincerity and genuineness from the adult. This is the one skill that is difficult to teach staff, which is why Max was even more of an asset in this sensitive situation. I knew he would be a great support not only to Chance but also to me.

Similar to Max, I had earned my place because I knew the youth's names. I'd praise them for positive things, casually, without making too big a deal (or then you wouldn't be cool) to offset the times when hard conversations would come. I wasn't Max, who was like a cool older brother or young uncle. I was more like an aunt who let them have fun, kept them safe, and held them accountable when needed. The ROCK is an environment where participants experience a touch of early independence. Fun, safety, and accountability are the pillars we use to ensure the best outcomes for our youth.

When Chance shared his pain and his plan with us, a foundation of trust was already established. That trust is also most likely why he decided to tell us. "Sure, let them all leave. Don't call my mom," Chance said after I'd suggested that he, Max, and I relocate to my office for a bit of privacy.

My request to move to the office wasn't a concern or unusual to him because small groups would often hang out in my far-from-pretentious space, where snacks abounded and you were safe to speak your mind. This also ensured visits to my office weren't just for instances of trouble. This way, being asked to step into my office didn't provoke additional anxiety or frustration.

Mom needed to be called, but I wanted Chance to make that

choice, as I was confident he would soon. If he refused or delayed too long, I would call her out of moral and legal obligation, but this is a crucial area regarding trust. If we lost his trust, the next time he or his friends faced a serious issue, they might not reach out to an adult. That very trust may have saved a life that night. As expected, Chance decided to call Mom in just a few minutes. Over the phone, I provided Mom with enough context for her to understand it was serious and needed to be addressed immediately, and I asked her to come alone.

Safety for our youth is the first priority at The ROCK, as it is for all adults in youth-facing roles. There are many ways to respond to serious situations, and we all find what works for us. Had I called Chance's mother without giving him the space to decide to make the call, that would not have been wrong because, again, the youth's safety is our first priority. I have found that when we have to make a serious decision, there is always a way to respect our youth's autonomy while never moving safety from the top of our list. What Chance shared with us was serious, and the fact that he had a means and a plan to execute it elevated my concern even more.

While we waited for Mom to arrive, we prompted Chance to share his story. We expressed empathy for how difficult his situation must be. We didn't take sides but validated the hurt he must be feeling. Eventually, Chance told his story. He lived most of the time with his mom and stepfather in a far from cohesive home. He felt Mom was getting bullied by her husband, and Chance wanted to protect her.

He also didn't see a future for himself, so he was determined to act now by saving his mom. This decision would take his life down a different road, ending in death or prison. But Chance was resolved. He didn't want to die, but he didn't want to live. Ending his own life after ending his stepfather's was what he had decided, despite how much he loved his mother. It was obvious that she loved him as well. They were living in a tough, blended family situation, but I had no idea how deep or serious the situation was.

When Mom was comfortable that Chance was safe and with a trusted adult, she and I sat together in a different office. She was visibly disturbed as she learned of the details. I empathized with her to my core as I, too, cared deeply for my children. Motherhood is hard, and sometimes you just need a listening ear. As she spoke, I listened. Meanwhile, Max continued to sit with Chance long after all the other participants and staff had left for the evening. The courage required for Max to sit in the uncomfortable moment with Chance, especially when he started crying, is invaluable. Not many would have been brave enough to stay in such a vulnerable place as Max did.

A little after midnight, Chance and Max joined Mom and me. Chance and his mother hugged, and emotions ran high: teenage anger and grief, along with a mother's fear, sense of failure, and her own grief overflowed. At The ROCK, we handle emotionally high situations like this as delicately as possible. We work with those involved to make sure they have a plan, including resources and referrals. Child protective services, community mental health professionals, and other appropriate professionals were engaged, as is common practice in these situations. In the case of Chance and Mom, I was determined to maintain a connection because I was both concerned and sincerely cared. I was elated when Mom gave me permission to call her over the weekend.

After Chance and Mom left, I asked Max if I could buy him a drink. Max slid onto a bar stool at the center's cafe, as I got each of us a soda and sat down to make sure Max was good. He'd just helped save a life, or possibly two, while doing a difficult job he loved. He built a relationship with a young person, which provided the opportunity and honor to sit in the muck. We toasted our plastic soda bottles and quietly reflected for a moment.

"You did a good job tonight. Are you okay?" I asked, breaking the silence.

He looked at me and asked, "What would have happened if we weren't here?" There was no quick or witty response from me. I didn't have one.

"I don't know. I have asked myself that more than once. We are fortunate to have been here and that Chance chose to come tonight. The connection you built with Chance made you that person he could trust. You are doing important work. By taking the time to ask a young man how he was doing, you opened the door to a life-changing conversation." That's all I had.

We finished our drinks, locked up the building, and went to our respective cars. As I drove home, I wondered if adults truly understand the importance of their roles in the lives of children. I considered opportunities taken and opportunities lost. And worse, I thought about the times when adults make it harder for kids by negating their feelings or neglecting to truly listen to them. As inundated as we are as adults with our own stressors, we must remember adolescence comes with its own challenges. Our youth deserve care and support from us in these moments. When we give them that, open and honest relationships have fertile ground in which to grow.

Not all moments are or appear to be as weighty as this one. Your work is essential, and you often don't realize the difference you make in a young person's life. It may be generations from now when the seed you planted sprouts to life, but it wouldn't have been without you.

Courage. Confidence. Connection. These qualities are developed in youth and are essential for adults willing to be in the moments with them. I shared Chance's story to illustrate what this can look like. While our approaches may differ from others, I believe there are effective ways to navigate difficult conversations and decisions with courage, confidence, and connection. Additionally, I share this story to highlight the importance of investing more in your people than in your programs. Discover You™, as impactful as it is, didn't prevent Chance from making a grave mistake. Max and his mother did, and ultimately, Chance made the right choice. Programs alone cannot cultivate youth who are capable of thriving when they can and struggling well when they need to. People do.

Chapter 4

Courage

"If one girl with courage is a revolution, imagine what feats we can achieve together."
— *Queen Rania of Jordan*

A complex world requires courage. The challenges we face are constantly evolving, and it takes courage to navigate through them with resilience and determination. It's not always easy, but if we're to be effective, courage is absolutely necessary.

Sometimes, fears are well-founded, keeping us from doing reckless things that could harm ourselves or others. Thus, fear should be respected for the role it plays in our lives. However, there is a required balance of fear and bravery because if you aren't mindful, fear can also be limiting and incapacitating.

Consider Grace and her fear. Grace was attending summer camp at The ROCK. The field trip for that week was to go to the water park. Grace was dreading the trip because she had a debilitating fear of water. For years, she had avoided going to the beach or pool parties. If she did go, she would find herself withdrawing from socializing. Even worse, she became anxious when her friends entered the water, despite them being strong swimmers. The pending field trip helped Grace choose to confront her fear, determined to enjoy the water park with her friends.

Grace and her father approached the program director with their concerns. Together, they developed a success plan that included appointing the program director, who understood the situation, as Grace's chaperone. They would evaluate risks and options throughout the day and make adjustments as necessary. At each activity, the pair discussed safety, and when Grace chose to enter the water, she did so alongside her chaperone. Throughout the day, they talked about how Grace was primarily afraid of being in deep water, but she wanted to be with her friends, making it important for her to overcome this fear. The trip marked Grace's first positive experience with water.

After successfully entering the water during the field trip, Grace decided to increase her confidence around water. She took swimming lessons and became a strong swimmer. She could still be apprehensive, but she had a better understanding of her limits and could identify when it was appropriate to fear water and when she could comfortably enjoy it.

Understanding the fear is the first step in increasing courage and becoming braver. Encourage young people to ask themselves what they are afraid of and why.

One thing to consider about fear is that many fears are valid and keep us safe. Grace wasn't a strong swimmer, so she was rightly afraid of deep water. That is logical. However, sometimes fears don't keep us safe; they only limit us. In Grace's situation, her being in shallow water wasn't putting her at risk, so that fear was one that could be faced. When safety is considered and determined not to be a factor, face the fear.

We're fortunate to witness children often overcoming their fears at The ROCK. Sometimes, walking through those doors is a fear. Take Austin, for instance.

On Tuesday, twelve-year-old Austin reluctantly followed his mother into the vast room where about 50 other middle school youth were busy doing an art project, playing a board game, or heading off to the gym for basketball. "It's going to be fine, Austin. I checked these folks out, and I think you are going to love it here," Mom tried to persuade him.

Austin turned his head and threw up in the garbage can in front of everyone. Mom looked meekly at the staff and apologized, explaining that he gets a little nervous around people. That concluded day one.

> Sometimes fears don't keep us safe; they only limit us.

On Wednesday, Austin hesitantly followed his mother into the same room with the same youth. Staff discreetly brought a trash can closer. "Hi, Austin," said Miranda, one of our staff members, warmly. "Are you going to hang out with us today?"

"I'm not sure. Mom has to run an errand, and I thought I might stay for a few minutes," he said as his gaze scanned the room. Miranda wondered if he was looking for jeers following yesterday's trash can incident.

"What do you like to do? Maybe I can introduce you around, and Mom can return in a few."

"I guess" was Austin's more-than-hesitant response.

Miranda exchanged a secret glance with Mom. "We got this. See you in a bit?"

Mom patted Austin on the shoulder and told him to call her if he needed her. Six months later, Mom and Austin recorded a video for the program, laughing about the first day. Then Austin ran off to play basketball and called out, "Don't rush back, Mom. I'm going to be a while."

I can only marvel at the amount of courage Austin required on day two and how that courageous choice changed the trajectory of his life. Remember how, in Chapter 2, we discussed the self-efficacy that's built after we accomplish a goal? That's what happened with Austin. From that point on, he had something to refer to when he encountered new situations that riled up the butterflies in his stomach.

We adults have to work to exercise courage, too. We encourage youth to step out and take chances, but we must also assess where we're holding back and who our lack of courage affects. As adults in positions of providing for youth, we must often be courageous in the face of adversity. Front-line staff working directly with youth often see the problems and potential solutions first.

When we witness challenges such as our youth becoming increasingly disengaged and disenchanted or reluctant learners not wanting to participate, we may be the only voice to speak for them. It requires tremendous courage to confront a system, relentlessly pursue the dream of a better future, and entertain the hope of achieving it. The bravest and most courageous people we know will often tell you they acted while being afraid. They didn't wait for their fears to pass; instead, they managed their fears, acted with them, and built their bravery.

Ambrose Redmoon said, "Courage is not the absence of fear, but rather the judgment that something else is more important." That mindset is what saved The ROCK. The center was at risk of being closed due to a lack of funding and leadership; the young people wanted it to stay, and the adults knew it was needed but were unsure how to save it. Knowing what was possible and what was at risk if those possibilities didn't materialize is what drove me to the center to check it out on that summer day in 2003. Discover You™ was created to build thriving assets in youth. We aimed to develop engaging and impactful programming alongside the center's physical space.

Fortunately, although the fear of insufficient resources continued, the vision to meet the needs of youth remained clear.

In the spring of 2009, I visited a gift shop in a small town in northern Michigan that was going out of business. I saw three plaques that quoted Disney. One read: "It's kind of fun to do the impossible." The second: "All it takes is faith, trust, and a little pixie dust" – Peter Pan. The third: "If you can dream it you can do it." At 75% off, my total came to $7.53. Though insignificant to my wallet, it was very significant to my vision.

Those three plaques remain in sight from my desk today. They have served as an ongoing source of inspiration. Our dream has always been comprised of vision and courage. We have remained willing to work hard toward something that has not yet been achieved. Courage has given rise to a movement that is transforming the lives of young people for the better, and for that, I will be forever grateful.

Equip · Inspire · Impact

- **When a fearful situation arises, encourage young people to be braver and evaluate their fears by asking themselves what they fear and why.**
- **Provide safe opportunities for youth to challenge fears.**
- **Be courageous and take healthy risks in youth development.**

SCARF Model

"Between stimulus and response there is a space. In that space is our power to choose our response. In our response lies our growth and our freedom."

— *Viktor E. Frankl*

The SCARF model was developed in 2008 by Dr. David Rock, the author and originator of the term "neuroleadership," in his paper "SCARF: A Brain-Based Model for Collaborating With and Influencing Others."

SCARF is an acronym for five domains influencing our behavior in social situations:

- **Status**: Sense of importance by social comparisons.
- **Certainty**: Ability to predict the future.
- **Autonomy**: Perception of control, freedom, and choice.
- **Relatedness**: Sense of belonging and connection.
- **Fairness**: Perception of transparency and justice.

When our **Status, Certainty, Autonomy, Relatedness,** or **Fairness** is threatened, we automatically default to a threat response. To better understand our threat triggers is to better understand how we and others react in situations perceived as potentially harmful or dangerous. As human beings, emotions are one of the most powerful tools and resources we possess, and are often the expressive reaction to our threat triggers. We are the creators of our emotions, and we can choose how we think, feel, act, and react to the people and circumstances around us.

We are in a constant state of making decisions, often below the level of conscious awareness. Our brains regularly ask, "Is this moment a potential opportunity, or is it a potential threat?" Thus, we stand in the present and predict the future. We anticipate what will happen before it happens. When awaiting a potential opportunity, we think, "Something good is about to happen." With a potential threat, we think, "Something bad is about to happen."

When we perceive an opportunity, we release positive neurotransmitters, such as serotonin, dopamine, and oxytocin, throughout our body. These neurotransmitters broaden our thinking, making us more creative and better at problem-solving. When we go down a threat path, we release cortisol, the stress hormone, which narrows and focuses our thinking and behavior to either "get in" and fight or "get out" and flee. Humans, like animals, move either toward a reward or away from a threat.

The SCARF model helps us consider what triggers a threat response. Dr. Rock's research shows that we activate threat mode when any of these five areas are called into question or jeopardized. However, our brains do not distinguish between a literal threat and a mental threat. When I mentioned the SCARF model earlier, you may have noticed the words "sense" or "perceived" were used in every definition. That means they are not necessarily physical threats.

> We are the creators of our emotions, and we can choose how we think, feel, act, and react to the people and circumstances around us.

This model is constructed around social situations. Even though those threats may be mental, they are still real and can cause us to be in a state of constant fight-or-flight, which is detrimental to our health and wellbeing.

SCARF provides language to assist us in labeling, understanding, or assessing threats. Additionally, the SCARF model provides a space between stimulus and response, allowing for a pause to develop an awareness of how negative thinking and self-talk influence us physically, emotionally, mentally, and behaviorally. This, in turn, can increase our awareness and understanding of these automatic negative thoughts and responses.

This process can help prepare young adults for the inevitable challenges they will face. We will now explore each domain of the SCARF model and consider what might trigger a threat response in young people. Concurrently, we will consider responses that youth can engage in to foster productive responses to those threats.

Status: Sense of importance by social comparisons
- Triggers
  - Becoming less or more popular
  - Social media comparisons
  - Not being chosen for a leadership position
- Productive responses
  - Encourage youth not to compare themselves to others
  - Review their strengths and values
  - Consider an action to move toward their preferred position

Certainty: Ability to predict the future
- Triggers
  - Facing a move or a new school
  - Parents divorcing
  - Household income drastically changing

- Productive responses
  - Discuss what is in their control and influence
  - List concerns about an issue and work through each concern
  - Take forward action when able

Autonomy: Perception of control, freedom, and choice
- Triggers
  - Lack of or removal of choice
  - Removal of privileges
  - Deadlines and assignments
- Productive responses
  - Provide opportunities for choice (for example, perhaps they need to do their homework on weeknights but can choose what time)
  - Allow safe natural consequences
  - Encourage self-expression

Relatedness: Sense of belonging and connection
- Triggers
  - Loneliness and disconnection
  - Losing a friend
  - Not feeling like they fit in
- Productive responses
  - Encourage joining clubs
  - Inspire the development of social skills
  - Promote teamwork and cooperation

Fairness: Perception of transparency and justice
- Triggers
  - Not getting a turn
  - Feeling like they are getting less
  - Being, or perceived to be, falsely accused

- Productive responses
  - Discuss the situation
  - Consider if there is an action or correction that can be taken
  - Engage problem-solving skills to seek a solution

Once I understood triggers, I realized why a young person might become enraged when someone moved in front of them in line. Their threat response is triggered, as they see the move as unfair. Their primal response that they are threatened is no different from adults becoming livid when someone behind them attempts to exit an airplane before them.

The SCARF model—**Status, Certainty, Autonomy, Relatedness**, and **Fairness**—is a powerful tool for helping us understand what may be causing strong reactions in our youth and ourselves. That awareness better prepares us to respond appropriately and constructively empower youth and understand their own.

Equip · Inspire · Impact

- **Understand your threat triggers as they relate to interacting with youth.**
- **Encourage youth to explore which component of SCARF is triggered when they experience a threat response.**
- **When threat responses are triggered, encourage youth to identify productive responses to them.**

Courageous Communication

"Non-violence is the greatest force at the disposal of mankind."

— *Gandhi*

Communication is a simple concept, yet it appears to be a challenge everywhere. Families, couples, co-workers, and institutions all seem to be grappling with communication difficulties.

In the 1960s, Dr. Marshall Rosenberg developed the nonviolent communication model. This model was designed to be an effective communication tool in challenging situations. Rosenberg grew up in an inner-city Detroit neighborhood during a violent time in our country's history. He was confronted daily with various forms of violence and was driven to find a solution to reduce it. Working with civil rights activists, Rosenberg developed and disseminated the nonviolent communication tool used to mediate between rioting students and college administrators. This model also contributed to the peaceful desegregation of public schools in long-segregated regions. Today, this peacemaking tool is used in over 60 countries to resolve personal, professional, and political differences, including those in business, education, government, and families.

Through Jose and his mother's experience, we will see how this simple and effective tool can build peace and cohesiveness in your world.

"I asked you to clean your room," sighed Mom. "I did," groaned Jose.

"This is clean?" she asked, looking around at clothes and gadgets strewn across the floor.

"Yes, I took out the trash and put my dirty clothes in the laundry," exclaimed Jose.

Sound familiar? Mom's and Jose's understanding of clean did not align and caused an unpleasant moment in their home. Let's examine how clear and direct communication can help resolve or prevent issues.

There are four components of nonviolent communication: **Observations**, **Feelings**, **Needs**, and **Requests**.

Observations: That which you can see or hear.
This can occur when you observe someone increasing the volume of their voice. Removing judgment words allows the observation to defuse a reactive or protective response from the receiver. Jose's mother, for instance, observed that there were clothes and gadgets on the floor after Jose said he'd cleaned his room, which is an effective approach. It would be ineffective to judge him by using words such as "lazy," "careless," and "disobedient".

Feelings: Emotions or body sensations.
In this application, your perceptions or interpretations should not reflect what you think or perceive someone is doing to you. This can be tricky, as we are often advised to leave our feelings out of things. It is important to recognize that both parties have feelings. After all, we're emotional beings. The critical component is in identifying our true

feelings. Mom might tell Jose that she feels frustrated or disappointed when his room is untidy.

Needs: What triggers feelings.

Our needs should remain free from blame or assigned worth. Let's say, for instance, like all of us, respect is one of Jose's needs. He told his mother he cleaned his room, but she didn't believe him and was talking more than listening. As a result, Jose feels disrespected. If he communicates his needs without eliminating the blame and inserts strategies first, he might respond with something like, "You never listen to me! Stop interrupting me while I'm talking!" Here, he's blaming his mom for failing to listen by telling her to stop interrupting him. Your needs are the beliefs and principles that are important in the way that you live and work. It is in the manifestation of what we need that we make our request or seek a desired outcome. Examples of needs include participation, stability, acceptance, safety, honesty, equality, etc.

Requests: Doable, concrete, specific, and affirmative actions. Requests are the final component of the nonviolent communication model. In this model, requests differ from demands and do not use fear, guilt, shame, manipulation, or reward. How do you feel when someone presents a request versus a demand? A request encourages cooperation and provides autonomy, whereas a demand incites a power dynamic. Phrases to frame requests can include: "Would you...?" "Could you...?" "It would help me if you would..." "It's supportive when...."

If Mom applied this model, her request after seeing Jose's room might be: "When I see clothes and other items on your floor (observation), I feel disappointed and disrespected (feeling), because I value you taking personal pride in our home (need). Will you please put away your clothes and other items when I ask you to clean your room (request)?" When Mom frames her request this way, it allows Jose to understand better why she's making this request and how this task would look when completed to her expectations.

> Clear communication does not have to be difficult, but it does require commitment and courage.

Clear communication does not have to be difficult, but it does require commitment and courage. Since the nonviolent communication tool is equally effective in affirming positive behaviors, you can practice using it regularly. For example, "I appreciate you picking up your clothes and other items when I ask you to clean your room. That makes me feel valued, respected, and proud of our home." The more you apply nonviolent communication, the more natural it will become. Initially, the language may feel rehearsed, but as you learn to use it, you will begin to put it into your own words and develop your own communication style.

Equip · Inspire · Impact

- **Remind youth of this form of communication by clearly posting the steps of nonviolent communication.**
- **Model nonviolent communication when you are interacting with youth.**
- **Use the nonviolent communication model in both positive and negative situations.**

Social Awareness

"You can make more friends in two months by becoming interested in other people than you can in two years by trying to get other people interested in you."

— *Dale Carnegie*

According to the Collaborative for Academic, Social, and Emotional Learning (CASEL), which is referenced in the Evidence-Based Frameworks section, social awareness is the ability to understand the perspectives of and empathize with others. This includes the capacity to feel compassion for others, understand broader historical and social norms for behavior in different settings, and recognize family, school, and community resources and supports. Social awareness is one of the five social and emotional skills that have been identified as key to success and fulfillment throughout our lives.

Social awareness is an essential skill to develop as it affects every aspect of our lives, personally and professionally. The most connected, accomplished, and confident people I know have high levels of social awareness. They know when to push forward, when to pivot, and when to step back. Learning this at an early age allows youth to adapt to social situations throughout their lives.

Critical components of social awareness, as identified by CASEL and other sources, include:

- **Empathy:** listening actively and grasping another person's perspective and feelings from verbal and nonverbal cues.
- **Respect for others:** to show regard for them and to value them.
- **Grace:** a belief that, in general, people are doing their best, and expecting the best of them.
- **Appreciation of diversity:** including getting along with people of different backgrounds and cultures.
- **Community or organizational awareness:** being aware of situations and identifying crucial social networks, and understanding the organizational forces at work, guiding values, and unspoken rules that operate among people.

Here are some quick examples that provide us with an increased understanding of what lacking social awareness skills looks like in practice. Dakota tells a joke and gets a laugh. He tells the same joke repeatedly until his peers get annoyed. Franklin distracts others by talking loudly during a movie. Kia wears shorts and a tank top to a formal wedding. Ryan runs and jumps at a theatrical play he is attending with his older brother. Lionel plays his music without headphones at the doctor's office.

The actions of these young people suggest they could benefit from developing their social awareness skills. As you assist youth in developing social skills, your response to their behavior depends on the age and maturity of the young person, with accountability taken into consideration. Setting clear expectations and consequences in advance is beneficial for all age groups. An initial response from many of these youth might be that they don't care what other people think. And they very well may not. However, addressing challenging social behaviors becomes more effective if the expectations and consequences are shared and agreed upon in advance. And, as in most situations, there must be follow-through to have a lasting impact.

For example, Ryan is five years old, running around at the play and being disruptive. His brother didn't anticipate the behavior, but now that it has started, it is clear something must change. For Ryan to stay

> Social awareness and high social skills enable more positive outcomes when interacting with others.

at the play, he must act like the other attendees, and Ryan's brother has to be specific about this in his expectations. To avoid disturbing the other attendees, Ryan's brother takes him outdoors until he chooses to participate acceptably, recognizing that they may need to leave.

More mature youth can be asked what they think they can gain from being socially aware and how it applies to their lives. Timely conversations and good questions share the knowledge that social awareness will help them throughout their lives to build connections with people, excel in their profession, and maneuver complex situations. Additionally, a lack of social awareness limits their ability to participate in many activities.

Opportunities to raise social awareness among our young people are abundant. People-watching is a pastime that many, including myself, enjoy, and it is one of the best ways to hone our social awareness skills. Encourage youth to observe people like a journalist would, being thoughtful and unbiased. Then, have youth privately share their observations. You can try the following scenarios and questions:

Observe two individuals and have them consider the following:

- What might each person be feeling? Why?
- What might their relationship be, and why do you think that?
- Does this appear to be a positive or negative interaction? Why?
- If you were to approach these two, how might you behave?

You can have youth observe a large group of people at a sporting event and consider:

- What are the expected or normal behaviors here?
- What would cause a negative disruption?
- How might you behave to enjoy a positive experience here?

Another option is to have young people consider their school:

- What are the expected behaviors or norms
  - In class?
  - In the lunchroom?
- What might you do to impact the class or lunchroom positively? Negatively?

By utilizing these opportunities, you can help youth explore various strategies for managing diverse situations. This will create an opportunity to provide feedback and encouragement, and help youth build a foundation for success in social situations.

Another component of social awareness is an understanding of the available resources. You can help youth build resource awareness by giving them a situation in which they might need help. Have them identify where they could go for help and who they might approach for assistance.

As the caring adult, offer suggestions of support as needed.

- At home
- School
- In your neighborhood

Social awareness and high social skills enable more positive outcomes when interacting with others. These skills can help young people be more courageous when connecting with others. You benefit youth when you model social awareness. Consider sharing instances where you have both successfully and unsuccessfully maneuvered social situations.

Equip · Inspire · Impact

- **Set clear expectations of behavior before entering social situations.**
- **Debrief the social awareness of characters when watching a movie.**
- **Provide feedback on social behaviors when appropriate.**

Chapter 5

Confidence

"As is our confidence, so is our capacity."
— *William Hazlitt*

Confidence is defined as a belief in yourself and your abilities. It looks much better when it is not paired with arrogance, which is an overbearing and presumptuous attitude of superiority. Some people unnecessarily avoid developing or displaying confidence to avoid appearing arrogant. Arrogance and confidence are vastly different concepts, as you can believe in yourself without feeling or behaving in a superior manner.

As caring adults, we can help young people develop confidence. Although we may initially have more confidence in them than they have in themselves, the goal is for young people to develop self-confidence and believe in their own abilities. Confidence precedes courage, as we first trust in ourselves and then summon the strength to act with courage. Like most of the strengths and traits we explore in this book, confidence is both innate and can be developed. Some people are predisposed to a confident nature or slant, while others not as much.

Our ROCK/Discover You™ team is comprised of individuals who hold many different roles. Collectively, we work to bring the organization's vision of "all youth having the opportunity to live their potential" to life. When asked what confidence in youth looks like, Jill, our ROCK Out-of-School Director, said, "A young person joining a new group, talking to staff and other adults, trying a new activity, speaking up, being authentic, and having an opinion they are willing to share."

Cindy, our Discover You™ Partnership Specialist, defined confidence in youth as "Having a fear of failure but stepping out and doing it anyway."

Tina, our Discover You™ Training Specialist, said confidence manifests itself "as a head held high; shoulders back; eye contact; and a willingness to step forward, speak up, and be still as needed."

Holly, our Discover You™ Administrator, added, "For a young person, it's sharing who they are with others, speaking out against bullies, participating in sports or band, and performing in front of others. When I think of confidence in youth, I can't help but picture a kid saying, 'Look what I can do.' It's a determined look and a fire in their eyes."

Kate, our Discover You™ Community Specialist, said, "Confidence is the ability to be at our best because we recognize our strengths and the value we bring to the world when using them. A young person with confidence has the ability to look others in the eye and offer a firm handshake. They are willing to risk embarrassment or failure by accepting new challenges that lead them closer to their goals."

Well said, team. Courageous actions, whether small and everyday or grand and once-in-a-lifetime, are directly a result of confidence. Many actions a young person takes require a degree of confidence. Confidence benefits both Mel, who plays soccer in eighth grade, and Max, who is entering post-secondary school.

Each must first believe in their ability to be successful. Confidence leads us into a functional future of healthy risk-taking, making friends, securing employment, and living life well.

Confidence is a result of many factors, including the development of social and emotional skills, the increase in Developmental Assets (as described in the Evidence-Based Frameworks section), and the enhancement of overall

> The level of confidence a young person develops will significantly influence their ability to reach their full potential.

wellbeing. Having a growth mindset, leveraging character strengths and strong relational skills, managing one's thoughts, grit, resilience, and positive emotions, and failing well all contribute to developing confidence.

Additionally, a strong support system can help build confidence. When baby Gloria is taking her first step, cheers and encouragement abound from her loving and supportive parents: "You can do this. We believe in you. You are so brave." Together, they are building confidence that will grow throughout her lifetime.

Developing confidence can also stem from past successes, which enable one to build self-efficacy and transfer a win from one situation to a belief in future successes. According to Angela Duckworth, the psychologist I referenced in Chapter 3 on grit, confidence is built when a young person witnesses evidence that they are on the right path. One way to experience that is by setting incremental goals that lead to a larger goal. Thus, your direction is evident, and your path is clear, as is your location on the path.

In this section, we saw how confidence is a by-product of skill development and how you can help foster confidence in the youth in your life. We also saw that there are times we hold the space for youth to become confident by leading with our confidence in them.

The level of confidence a young person develops will significantly influence their ability to reach their full potential.

Equip · Inspire · Impact

- **Create a culture of failing well to ensure setbacks do not undermine confidence.**
- **Express your confidence in young people openly as they develop their own.**
- **Help youth build confidence by acknowledging and celebrating incremental wins.**

Emotional Intelligence

"And now that you don't have to be perfect, you can be good."

— *John Steinbeck*

Emotional intelligence is the ability to understand and manage our emotions effectively and positively, which leads us toward our goals and desired future. It is a key component in social and emotional learning (SEL). In Chapter 1, we explored positive emotions, and in the following section, we will examine the process of partnering with challenging emotions. Here, we will consider the overall importance of emotional intelligence.

Emotions trigger chemical and physical reactions in our bodies. They are messy, complex, confusing, subjective, and hard to avoid, describe, and manage. Okay, so what do we do with all of that? Together, we will develop an understanding of emotions and a working relationship with them.

Emotions move us through situations, acting like a GPS and radar system combined. They both warn and direct, inform and confuse. Emotions are influenced by our past, our fears, and our biases. That combination causes them to be unreliable, making it best not to believe everything you feel. The strong sensations caused by these emotions or feelings can cause intense reactions. Some choose to suppress their emotions, some medicate them, and some act on them (occasionally to their detriment), while others navigate their emotions well.

Consider Savannah's current level of emotional intelligence. Savannah seems to share every emotion she has with anyone in her vicinity. She is in despair over what is for dinner, in love over a puppy, in rage over not

> Emotional intelligence is a pivotal concept in youth shifting from emotional reactions to intentional choices.

getting an outfit she wants, overwhelmed with schoolwork, and in anguish over not being invited to a party. These regular and intense reactions are wearing on her relationships. Savannah and those around her could benefit from her development of emotional intelligence and growth in self-awareness and self-management. Though her emotions are valid, how she views them and the influence she allows them to have on her behavior could be navigated more effectively.

Instead of emotions controlling Savannah and others, how about helping young people learn to navigate life with them as a trusted friend by their side? Dr. Susan David, psychologist and author of *Emotional Agility*, suggests we regard emotions as data, not directives. This allows emotions to be felt and reviewed while reducing their impact on one's behavior.

The simple idea of viewing emotions as data instead of directives changed how I viewed my own emotions and influenced how I see others around me handling theirs. When our emotions direct or dictate our actions, we fall victim to the whims of ourselves as well as others. It may be understandable for a toddler to respond with a tantrum over the despair he feels from not receiving a treat.

However, when an adolescent reacts in this way, it is evident that there is a lack of emotional awareness and management.

David's focus on emotional agility identifies four core aspects that assist in gaining emotional awareness and management: **Showing Up**, **Stepping Out**, **Walking Your Why**, and **Moving On**.

Showing Up: Experiencing all of your emotions, being present with and aware of them.

This conveys the idea that one might benefit from interacting with, not avoiding, their emotions. Here, we can encourage young people to face their thoughts, emotions, and behaviors willingly, and with curiosity and kindness. Emotions are valid, though not always an accurate representation of a situation. Once youth learn how to partner with emotions, they can move forward more effectively in situations.

Stepping Out: Shifting perspective, detaching from the emotions, and observing them like watching a movie or another's behavior.

We can explain this to our youth by suggesting they consider that emotions are just emotions. "Just emotions" removes power from those feelings, creates space for them to choose how to respond, and equips young people with personal control. Using the language "just emotions" does not give permission to trivialize or belittle another's emotions or tell them it isn't okay to feel what they are feeling. As mentioned earlier, emotions are complex and are not facts, but rather feelings. We perceive things differently depending on the day, our mood, or our circumstances. The goal is that our emotions inform us, rather than control us.

Walking Your Why: Embracing the principles of living in alignment with one's values. Here, young people can reflect on their core values and goals, which we explore in greater depth in Chapter 7. They can combine their feelings, emotions, and thoughts with what they want from life and manage them toward that goal.

Moving On: Making small, deliberate tweaks in our behavior.

At this point, I'd conduct the Learning Loop that we explored in Chapter 3 and encourage young people to reflect on what went well, what they struggled with, and what they might do differently next time. This evaluation empowers them to make more informed decisions in the future. But do move on. Our youth can adjust habits and behaviors as necessary, try to adjust their reactions, and then move forward. New emotions, such as guilt and anxiety, may arise from the young person's original emotional reactions. Should that happen, they can restart the process as often as needed while still moving forward.

Increasing our emotional vocabulary helps us understand and express emotions more effectively. There are many more emotions than happiness, fear, or anger, which tend to be our go-to emotions. Brené Brown identifies 88 different emotions in her book *Altas of the Heart*. For example, young people may say they are angry, but perhaps they actually feel disgusted, self-righteous, or hateful. They may say they are happy, but are they feeling joy, relief, contentment, or gratitude? The more specific youth can be on what they are feeling, the easier it is to explore those feelings and the more sense they begin to make. Using a broader emotional vocabulary provides the foundation for a beneficial conversation surrounding emotions.

EMOTIONAL VOCABULARY

FEAR

- **Scared**
  - Helpless
  - Frightened
- **Anxious**
  - Overwhelmed
  - Worried
- **Insecure**
  - Inadequate
  - Inferior
- **Weak**
  - Worthless
  - Insignificant
- **Rejected**
  - Excluded
  - Persecuted
- **Threatened**
  - Nervous
  - Exposed

SORROW

- **Lonely**
  - Isolated
  - Abandoned
- **Vulnerable**
  - Victimized
  - Fragile
- **Despair**
  - Grieving
  - Powerless
- **Guilty**
  - Ashamed
  - Remorseful
- **Depressed**
  - Empty
  - Inferior
- **Hurt**
  - Disappointed
  - Embarrassed

SURPRISE

- **Startled**
  - Shocked
  - Dismayed
- **Confused**
  - Disillusioned
  - Perplexed
- **Amazed**
  - Astonished
  - Awed
- **Excited**
  - Eager
  - Energized

DISGUST

- **Disapproving**
  - Judgmental
  - Embarrassed
- **Disappointed**
  - Appalled
  - Revolted
- **Awful**
  - Nauseated
  - Detestable
- **Repelled**
  - Horrified
  - Hesitant

HAPPY

- **Playful**
  - Amused
  - Cheeky
- **Content**
  - Free
  - Joyful
- **Proud**
  - Successful
  - Confident
- **Accepted**
  - Respected
  - Valued
- **Powerful**
  - Courageous
  - Self-reliant
- **Peaceful**
  - Loving
  - Thankful
- **Trustful**
  - Sensitive
  - Intimate
- **Optimistic**
  - Hopeful
  - Inspired

ANGER

- **Let Down**
  - Betrayed
  - Resentful
- **Humiliated**
  - Disrespected
  - Ridiculed
- **Bitter**
  - Indignant
  - Violated
- **Mad**
  - Furious
  - Jealous
- **Aggressive**
  - Provoked
  - Hostile
- **Frustrated**
  - Infuriated
  - Annoyed
- **Distant**
  - Withdrawn
  - Numb
- **Critical**
  - Skeptical
  - Dismissive

BAD

- **Bored**
  - Indifferent
  - Apathetic
- **Busy**
  - Pressured
  - Rushed
- **Stressed**
  - Overwhelmed
  - Out of Control
- **Tired**
  - Sleepy
  - Unfocused

Good conversation starters include:

- What specific emotion did you experience?
- Did you use the emotion as data or a directive? How?
- Where did the emotion come from, and why did you react that way?
- Have you done a Learning Loop?

Emotional intelligence is a pivotal concept in youth shifting from emotional reactions to intentional choices. Emotions cycle constantly; remind them of this. As youth become more emotionally intelligent, they will likely consider emotions differently. When our youth partner with their emotions, instead of immediately reacting, they can place distance between themselves and the emotion and take time to consider these emotions. You can help youth partner with their emotions by encouraging them to:

- Be curious as to why they are feeling what they are feeling. Review the list of emotions mentioned earlier to help youth specifically name their feeling. For instance, there is a difference between feeling sad and feeling wronged.
- Be compassionate with themselves and provide grace. For example, youth could allow themselves to feel wronged even though they don't logically see that emotion as appropriate in a situation.
- Use emotions to their advantage. Youth can objectively understand that emotions are information and that their current situation might be causing them to experience more extreme emotions than what benefits them.

Emotional intelligence is a skill many of us work on throughout our lives, and it continues to develop as we mature. Starting young provides youth with a significant advantage. The ability to view emotions as data to inform us, rather than as facts to control us, allows for greater success in managing emotions.

Equip · Inspire · Impact

- **Encourage youth to increase their emotional vocabulary to describe emotions accurately.**
- **Teach youth to dismantle and explore their emotions and consider why they might be feeling a particular way.**
- **When youth experience a strong emotion, ask them what data that emotion is providing them.**

Partnering with Challenging Emotions

"Each moment is a choice. No matter how frustrating or boring or constraining or painful or oppressive our experience, we can always choose how we respond."

— *Marc Brackett*

Many emotions, such as anger, despair, grief, and loneliness, are labeled as negative. They don't make us feel positive and can pull us in unproductive directions. Are they truly negative, though? Not necessarily. Emotions aren't like electric charges that are either positive or negative. They are more complex than that, as these challenging emotions are beneficial and provide information, like emotions labeled as positive.

Uncomfortable or challenging emotions are often signs of something not going right. When we respond appropriately and with forethought, we can process our emotions and let them pass. Emotions themselves are neither good nor bad; it is what you do with them that matters.

The more we help young people understand and name their emotions, and delve deeply into them, the better they will be able to partner with the spectrum of emotions to build their best lives. Life, for no one, will be continually happy and positive. Trying to outrun and avoid life's challenges is exhausting and inevitably impossible. Yet, avoiding non-positive emotions is where we spend a lot of energy. Young people will experience endless benefits as they learn to navigate the complexity of the emotions that come with life, and those benefits will continue to compound as they move into their future.

The opposite is true when young people attempt avoidance. Their opportunity to be prepared for challenges is lessened. In Chapter 3, we explored how it is not the caring adult's job to insulate our youth from real-life

> Emotions themselves are neither good nor bad; it is what you do with them that matters.

experiences, including negative emotions. We must avoid shielding our youth by problem-solving for them, as these experiences will help them be better prepared to navigate through life.

When youth identify the emotions they are feeling, they should be cautious not to take them on as a definition of who they are. They may be feeling anger, but they are not an angry person. That is an important distinction for young people. As adults, we must be cautious of labels we might impose on youth that can become part of their identity and stick with them for a lifetime. Keeping emotions at a healthy distance can allow youth to see them as something fluid, not concrete, permanent, or unchangeable.

Some of the challenges we hear many of our young people commonly express are related to stress, anxiety, depression, and being overwhelmed. It would be beneficial to help them understand that, though situations are difficult, it is not necessarily the actual situation causing those feelings, but how the individual chooses to respond. This understanding can better equip them to manage and work with the situations they are reacting to with stress, anxiety, or other challenging emotions. Note an important distinction here: this is a broad statement that does not negate mental health diagnoses or severe stress, anxiety, or depression.

We can explore emotional responses in youth with Nathaniel, who considers himself an angry ninth-grade student and is quick to tell you that. He proudly declares, "I have anger issues" and considers that permission to be explosive, rude, and uncooperative. He chooses to be negative about school, a vacation, his parents, his sister, and most generally, everything he encounters. Nathaniel has taken an emotion that is easily accessible to him and built his identity around it.

Many youth, including Nathaniel, could benefit from developing a partnership with these negative emotions. Developing a sense of personal responsibility around controlling and understanding these negative emotions and how they can better manage these emotions would be a solid start to taking control.

Negative emotions, including stress or anger, don't necessarily come from the situation but from our emotional response to it. It is significant for youth to be able to say that it's not the situation that is stressful, but their response to the situation. They may not be able to change a situation, but they can change their response to it. Youth can face a difficult situation and respond by saying either "I am feeling stressed" or "I am not feeling stressed."

Although we often don't think positively about stress, it does have its benefits. For one thing, it alerts us to be aware of situations. It tells us something isn't right. When youth view the situation as a challenge rather than a threat, they can utilize their body's responses to move forward. They can use self-efficacy to remind themselves that they have handled similar situations before and can handle this one as well.

When we face harmful or stressful situations, we experience various responses that include:

- **Fight-or-flight response:** Our bodies experience an influx of chemicals that can motivate and energize us, preparing us to defend against or flee from the perceived threat.
- **Freeze response:** Our bodies become unable to react, leaving us immobile or unresponsive.
- **Fawn response:** This is a stress response that causes one to attempt to please others to avoid conflict.
- **Challenge response:** Views stress as an opportunity for growth and development. We can partner with our stressors, and our performance is enhanced.
- **Bigger-than-self response:** Alerts us to the need to reach out to others for help.
- **Resilience response:** When we see these situations as opportunities to become stronger, we become more flexible in our reactions.

When youth learn to insert space between the stressful or negative trigger and their reaction, they can respond to the situation intentionally, increasing the likelihood of getting closer to the desired outcome. Youth also have an option to reframe stress and other negative emotions, similar to the ability to reframe other situations, which was explored in Chapter 1. This can improve health, equip them with better coping strategies, and result in fewer negative repercussions.

According to Dr. Michelle McQuaid, co-creator of the Learning Loop, people who consistently thrive also experience negative emotions. In her opinion, it is inevitable to encounter difficulties, challenges, and pain in a world so complex.

You can assist youth in facing, not avoiding, challenging emotions by:

- properly naming and understanding emotions.
- recognizing that emotions are fleeting and not necessarily an accurate account of a situation.
- using emotions as information to make better decisions, not feelings that derail decisions.

Emotions, positive or negative, comfortable or uncomfortable, are best when managed and not avoided. Youth can benefit from partnering with challenging emotions in multiple ways. Using them as data can inform better decision-making, understanding the actual emotions can provide clarity, and recognizing that young people have a choice in how they respond to their emotions is empowering. Youth can develop the strengths and characteristics needed to navigate emotional distress, gaining the confidence to manage life's inevitable ups and downs.

Equip · Inspire · Impact

- **When dealing with challenging emotions, encourage youth to find a productive outlet, such as going for a walk or exercising.**
- **Encourage youth to face, not avoid, challenging emotions.**
- **Encourage framing emotions as something youth feel, not something they are.**

Beyond Your Comfort Zone

"Life begins at the end of your comfort zone."
— *Neale Donald Walsch*

A comfort zone is a safe space where we feel secure and content, whether physically, emotionally, or a combination of both. Have you ever wondered why we seek comfort and avoid discomfort? As a species, we have survived by avoiding things that threaten us and gravitating to things that ensure our ability to survive and thrive. Common sense and reason dictate we seek shelter as needed, avoid extreme temperatures, and meet our basic needs, including food and water.

When safety is not a factor, the desire to remain in a state of comfort can be limiting and lead to missed opportunities. For our youth, this could manifest as being afraid to try out for a team or join a club, or an unwillingness to try new foods. As so much of life lies outside of our comfort zone, it is important to push past it. Together, we explore the need to move beyond fears and limits, embrace a growth mindset, and encourage our youth to get uncomfortable.

Alexia's story illustrates the limitations of a comfort zone. She was so averse to discomfort that she found herself in a state of inaction. Unemployed and losing hope after graduating from high school with aspirations of becoming a welder, Alexia didn't know where to start. She faced multiple challenges that made her extremely uncomfortable and felt stuck. While aware that she needed to continue her education and find gainful employment, she was uncertain about how to secure financing for classes. Moreover, Alexia was unsure about which school to attend. Living independently, she was solely responsible for paying her bills, and her need for immediate income made a lengthy college welding program unfeasible.

Incremental change, such as doing one uncomfortable thing every day, can transform the world by providing options that were never considered.

Alexia had always disliked being in unfamiliar situations where she wasn't comfortable, so it was significant for her to step out of her comfort zone and reach out to me for help. One by one, we explored her list of concerns and found a workable solution together, allowing Alexia to enroll in a trade school for the next term. She was still uncomfortable the day she started welding school, but through the process, she had grown in her ability to be comfortable with being uncomfortable. She faced many new challenges as she progressed through the next steps, including the first test, new instructors, graduation, and interviews. Having expanded her comfort zone, she pushed through each uncomfortable moment, and her whole world began to open up. She is now a successful welder with gainful employment. Beyond her career, she continually finds opportunities to push beyond her comfort zone. Alexia found peace with being uncomfortable.

When you are helping young people get comfortable being uncomfortable, try these tactics:

- Suggest they pay attention to how they are feeling. What and where is the discomfort? Is it dread? Fear? Boredom?
- Challenge them to consider why they are feeling that way and challenge those feelings.
- Inquire:
  - Are they legitimate concerns?
  - Are they permanent or temporary?
  - What can youth do to manage them?
  - Is this a situation where they can, or perhaps should, push through?
- Find someone who appears comfortable and model their behavior. The keyword is "appears," as they may be every bit as uncomfortable as the young person is.
- Find someone who appears more uncomfortable and assist them. Skills and confidence are gained when helping others.
- Be available to debrief the wins and the challenges because when youth step into the unknown, they ultimately will face both.

Living inside a comfort zone can be equated to living inside self-imposed boundaries. It limits one's opportunities and experiences, often unnecessarily. Incremental change, such as doing one uncomfortable thing every day, can transform the world by providing options that were never considered. It can be as simple as complimenting someone at school or the grocery store, or verbally speaking instead of just waving to neighbors. Often, once in a situation, it becomes more comfortable, but even when it doesn't, remind the young person that no one knows they are uncomfortable except them. Being comfortable with being uncomfortable can become fun, and eventually, there are fewer uncomfortable things to worry about.

Equip · Inspire · Impact

- **Evaluate and challenge situations that feel uncomfortable, determine where the discomfort lies, and create tactics to address each concern.**
- **Challenge a young person to do one uncomfortable thing every day.**
- **Keep a journal to capture uncomfortable actions that were taken and their outcomes.**

SMART Plus Goal Setting

*"Setting goals is the first step in turning
the invisible into the visible."*

— *Tony Robbins*

In *Alice in Wonderland*, the somewhat lost and confused Alice approaches the cheeky Cheshire Cat and asks, *"Would you tell me, please, which way I ought to go from here?"*

"That depends a good deal on where you want to get to," said the Cat, *sporting a mischievous grin.*

"I don't much care where…," said Alice.

"Then it doesn't matter which way you go," said the Cat.

"…so long as I get SOMEWHERE," Alice added as an explanation. *"Oh, you're sure to do that,"* said the Cat, *"if you only walk long enough."*

This profoundly sums up the experience many of our young people are facing. They are being asked to make critical life choices and follow paths leading to unknown destinations. Years later, they realize they have arrived somewhere, but aren't sure where, why, or how they got there.

Goal setting involves developing an action plan designed to motivate and guide an individual or group toward a specific objective. Goals are more deliberate than desires and momentary intentions. Therefore, setting goals means a person has committed thought, emotion, and behavior toward attaining the goal.

Goal setting has many advantages. For some, it helps them identify and name their priorities. For others, it provides a concrete measurement. Goals can be written, clearly defined, and formal, or they can remain ambiguous and flexible.

The process of intentional goal setting enables youth to identify what is important to them and create a plan to achieve it, providing a filter for making informed decisions that impact their future.

Setting goals can help many of us, but it doesn't come easily for everyone. At Discover You™, we use the concept of SMART goals. A SMART goal is an intentional process that enables young people to identify actionable steps in a sequence. We have added a few steps, the Plus, to help youth develop tangible goals that are supported by a real-life plan.

The **SMART** acronym stands for:

- **Specific**
- **Measurable**
- **Approach**
- **Realistic**
- **Time-bound**

Heather's example demonstrates SMART Plus goals. She is a dedicated 11th-grade student who is determined to attend and ultimately graduate from her parents' alma mater. This university is renowned for its rigorous admissions process, which accepts only those with high grade point averages and candidates who demonstrate a strong commitment to excellence. Heather uses the SMART Plus goal model to create an actionable plan for success.

Specific: Heather's goal could be to "go to university," but in her instance, she can be more specific than that. Heather's goal is to "Attend the University of ABC."

Measurable: Heather can measure this by being accepted into the university and enrolling in classes.

Approach: Goals should be formulated in a way that encourages approach, rather than avoidance. Having something to work toward is mentally easier than working to avoid something. In this instance, it is clear that University ABC is where Heather wants to go. An example to demonstrate the approach concept may be "I want to attend University ABC," which is an approach style, versus "I don't want to attend schools X, Y, and Z," which is the avoidance style. We aspire toward what we say, making it advantageous to think about what we prefer to happen.

Realistic: It is realistic for Heather to attend University ABC, based on available information.

Time-bound: The goal should be linked to a definite time frame. Heather plans to attend University ABC in the fall after graduating from high school. Heather added a time constraint to her goal and is now ready for part two.

"I will attend the University of ABC in the fall immediately following high school graduation."

When young people create a SMART goal, a few additional considerations will make their goals even more achievable. We leverage the following steps with our youth at The ROCK: **Motivation**, **Primers**, **Action Items**, **Plan B**, **Accountability**, **Commitment**, **Celebration**, and **Maintenance**.

Motivation: Direct the youth to capture their why. Why is this goal important? What motivates them to achieve this goal? The ability to revisit the inspiration behind setting the goal can help keep youth on track and motivated to push forward when difficult times arise. Heather's motivation might be to build a future for herself that reflects her childhood. Her parents' education provided a fulfilling environment growing up, one she would like to replicate for her future children.

Primers: Primers are conscious or unconscious cues that remind our youth of the goal or their motivation behind it. Heather's primer could be a bracelet with the university name on it or an image of the mountains where she intends to live and work upon completing her university studies. Using highly visible primers can keep goals at the forefront, helping youth stay focused on what they need to accomplish.

Action items: Young people should list specific actions they will take to achieve their goals. These should be specific tactics they intend to deploy to move them in that direction. Heather's action items might include applying to the university, touring the campus, studying a certain amount of time, or maintaining a minimum GPA.

Plan B: Youth should always have a Plan B. This is a predetermined plan for actions they can take when things don't go as expected. With any goal they create, challenges will probably arise along the way. It is always a good idea for them to have an alternate plan to achieve their goals, just in case. Heather may need a plan if one of her class grades drops below the required GPA, such as checking in with a teacher. Heather may also want to apply to her second through fifth university choices, just in case something happens with her first choice.

Accountability: Encourage the use of an accountability partner to help keep young people on track. They are far more likely to be successful if they have someone to hold them accountable. In this instance, Heather's accountability partner might be her parents, a trusted teacher, or another responsible individual who shares her desire for success.

Commitment: Reaching their goals requires commitment. Young people can find ways to reinforce or remind themselves why this is important. They should start by writing down their goals and perhaps signing a contract with themselves.

Celebration: Both small and large successes should be celebrated. If it's a long journey to reach the ultimate goal, build in mini-goals with wins to celebrate along the way. Achieving both smaller and ultimate goals shows young people what they are capable of. Setting and achieving high goals builds pride, self-respect, self-efficacy, and resilience skills. The positive emotions of celebration help reinforce the change and increase motivation. Heather might choose to celebrate each grade she gets, her acceptance letters, or the end of a successful semester.

Maintenance: After the goal is achieved, challenge young people to make a maintenance plan so they don't lose the progress they made when they achieved this goal. For Heather, once she gets to university, she will want to maintain her status. This could include new goals as part of her maintenance plan. Heather might include maintaining a specific GPA or achieving a minimum number of credits per semester, and determining a graduation date.

Developing good habits of goal setting can benefit youth in many ways. Goals can provide a filter for them to enlist when presented with choices. Try adding a series of questions to the goal sheet that the young person can ask themselves when opportunities arise. Does this opportunity:

- Put me closer to or farther from my goal?
- Help me achieve my goal?
- Align with what I want for my life?

Developing SMART Plus goals provides various support for our youth. The process of intentional goal setting enables youth to identify what is important to them and create a plan to achieve it, providing a filter for making informed decisions that impact their future. Goal setting also reminds young people that achieving many of the important things in life requires hard work and close attention.

Equip · Inspire · Impact

- **When young people share their hopes and dreams, encourage them to turn them into SMART Plus goals.**
- **Whether the goal is formal or informal, encourage young people to identify an alternate plan of action should the unexpected arise.**
- **Encourage young people to consider if unrelated opportunities align with their long-term goals.**

Chapter 6

Connection

"Relationships are all there is. Everything in the universe only exists because it is in relationship to everything else. Nothing exists in isolation."

— *Margaret J. Wheatley*

Connection. To be connected is to be in relationship. Thriving and struggling well requires our youth to be equipped to successfully manage relationships in broad settings with many individuals across various roles. Youth need a variety of connections, including positive peer relationships, healthy partner relationships, and Developmental Relationships (as explored in the Evidence-Based Frameworks section) with key caring adults. Relationships are integral to life as we are, by nature, relational creatures.

This chapter primarily focuses on fostering connection and exploring the impact of loneliness. Loneliness is to be out of connection and is an epidemic. The problem is pervasive. The U.S. Surgeon General's advisory report found that loneliness increases the risk of premature death by 26% and isolation by 29%. Recent events are credited as a significant contributing factor, while social media continues to add to the phenomenon. The more time you spend on social media, the less time you spend having real-life connections. It also weakens your social skills and throws you into a vicious cycle of craving connection, which you feed by scrolling, ultimately distancing you from genuine connection. Social media "likes" and "friends" do not offset loneliness in the real world.

The need for connection is undeniably real and easier to ignore than fix. Like many societal problems, the solution is complex, requiring time and resources.

Building connections and reducing loneliness requires intentional work; here are a few ways to do that.

- **Build social confidence.** Our youth are experiencing diminished social skills that we cannot assume they will learn independently. Teach them and provide space for youth to master these skills.
- **Encourage participation.** Help youth find areas of interest and join in-person groups.
- **Utilize out-of-school-time programs.** Just because your young person is mature enough to be home alone doesn't mean there aren't better options. Encourage them to be with their peers in positive environments.
- **Put devices down.** Adults must put ours down first. When we are in physical proximity with someone and engaged in a screen, rather than the world around us, we are contributing to our own and the world's loneliness. Youth and our world need us to be present.

Zach provides us with a wonderful opportunity to explore youth-based loneliness. Zach feels isolated. He won't say he is lonely. Maybe he doesn't even know it, but he is. He attends school most days but utilizes the remote option when possible. He says hi to people in the halls when he feels he must, and sometimes

> Connection and relationships can be challenging to develop and maintain, but they are central to us as humans and critical to the quality of our lives.

they say hi back. The other students are on their phones when they can be and avoid eye contact when they aren't. The adults around him don't see the problem because he isn't showing outward signs of distress. When Zach goes home, his family asks about his day and genuinely cares about him.

"It was fine" is his three-word response as he heads to his room.

Zach's parents think he's either content or uninterested in them, so they give him his space. When there is a sit-down meal, which is rare, conversations seem awkward, responses are brief, and eventually, everyone finds a reason to engage with their phone or watch television. And they are all feeling lonely, lost, and disconnected. Mom suggests game night, fully expecting it to be shut down.

"That's lame," replied Zach. But when he sees Mom's disappointment, he says, "I'll give it a try. Once."

The family begins with a game night and builds opportunities from there. They start to laugh and decide that a few rules for their time together would be helpful. Mom and Dad set the example and put down their phones, which provides space for conversation and interaction, and a connection begins to build. Through family game night, Zach is developing social skills and confidence with his family that he can transfer to joining a club and making friends. Those skills include active listening, empathy, awareness of body language, and so much more. Connection and relationships can be challenging to develop and maintain, but they are central to us as humans and critical to the quality of our lives.

Equip · Inspire · Impact

- Starting with our youth, choose to engage with the people and environment around you.
- Practice spending less time on your own devices so that you model quality connections with the young people around you.
- Provide activities that promote youth interaction, such as volunteering, playing board games, or attending events.

Conversations and Communication

"Whatever words we utter should be chosen with care for people will hear them and be influenced by them for good or ill."

— *Buddha*

Conversations and communication are similar, as they both involve the exchange of ideas, and the two words are often used interchangeably. Conversations are always multi-directional, with two or more people engaged, whereas communication can be sent out in one direction but still must be received by the intended audience. Conversations tend to feel more informal, an exchange between friends, loved ones, or acquaintances. Communication often feels more formal and rigid and can lack active engagement. There is an art to both forms of interchange, as it is in our words and interactions with others that we help or harm. We explored one nuance of communication as a form of conflict resolution in Chapter 4, Nonviolent Communication.

Communication can be exceptionally challenging under certain circumstances. One scenario is when one party isn't invested in the communication. We can communicate the most precise and concise message, but it can be ineffective and frustrating if the other party isn't listening or participating. I often hear of this dynamic as a common school problem. The leader or teacher will say, "I sent out several emails, put dates and details in the newsletter, posted the information on the wall in the common area, and the students are telling me they didn't know what was going on. I don't know what else to do."

One of the key problems is that it appears the teacher is the only one participating in the communication. Communication involves participation from both sides. Often, the information distributor is held responsible for its ineffectiveness, but that is not always the case. A teacher may provide specific instructions to their students, only to be told the students have no idea what she is talking about. However, she is not solely responsible for the communication exchange. The students are as well. Unless it is a priority for the teacher and the student, the problem will persist. And it appears to be a greater priority for the teacher than for the students.

With a bit of intention, we can foster deep connections with young people and sustain those connections.

Similarly, I once overheard a son tell his mother she failed to communicate an event to him. She informed him it was on a full-page note on the refrigerator. In large print. Where he goes to get his morning juice. He had to move the note to open the door and get his juice, so he wouldn't miss it.

He missed it.

Communication can be improved when the recipient understands the importance of receiving the message and accepts responsibility for such. It is the receiver being intrinsically motivated to glean the information. That is, what is in it for them?

We are all motivated by personal gain. If the gain is only for the one communicating, you are entering a long-term, uphill, never-ending battle. On the contrary, when the receiver has a vested interest, they will seek out the information and ask questions if they don't understand. If that interest is lacking... you know how it goes. One key to communication is to frame it in a way that the intended receiver will want or even need to hear it.

Effective communication begins with good messaging. It should be clear, correct, complete, concise, and compassionate. Make sure it's easy to understand, conveys what you intended to say, including all the required information, is direct and to the point, and maintains awareness of the recipient's feelings and capacity. You also want to ensure that your environment is conducive to effective communication. Is the area too loud or distracting, preventing either party from engaging? Timing is another consideration to ensure the receiver is in a state to participate. You might not have their attention if they are in a hurry or dealing with something else. Another big consideration is to assume positive intent. Give the benefit of the doubt. For example, it's hard to decipher what tone is being used in a text exchange. Assumptions are often detrimental to the communication process. Finally, be mindful of your responses. Quick responses have yielded more apologies than well-thought-out ones.

Some research suggests that our response to someone's good news is just as important as our response to their bad news. Positive psychologist Shelly Gable developed a theory about how humans respond to positive news. In her theory, there are four ways of responding when a person shares good news with us: **active constructive**, **passive constructive**, **active destructive**, and **passive destructive**.

In our Discover You™ training, we do an active constructive responding (ACR) activity with adults, which tends to be quite enlightening. It is visible on their faces when they realize occasions on which they could have communicated better when receiving good information.

Simon excitedly shared, "I made the team!"

Ms. Owen, a favorite teacher, responded in an **active** and **constructive** manner by using a positive tone and engaging body language, and replied, "That is great! I know how hard you worked. Tell me more, and let's celebrate."

Dad displayed a **passive constructive** response. He was focused on his phone, did not make eye contact, and answered flatly, "That's good news."

Mr. D, an after-school staff member, responded in an **active destructive** manner. Between his closed posture and deflated tone, he was obviously frustrated when he said, "That sounds like a big commitment. How can you possibly do it with everything you have going on? You will probably fail science now."

Ms. Sandy, the bus driver, was **passive** and **destructive** in her response. She stared at her paperwork and said, "Did you pick up the trash?"

Which adult do you think Simon wants to have a conversation with? Who do you want to chat with? I'm sure Ms. Owen is the adult Simon will turn to with both his good and bad news in the future. Her willingness to celebrate with him creates a strong foundation of trust.

Whenever I do this exercise, I am reminded of the times when I haven't done my best. More importantly, it renews my commitment to communicating better in the future. As adults, we can reflect on when we are better communicators, as often it is at the end of our day, when we are tired and have given our all, that we tend to respond less favorably. With a bit of intention, which we'll discuss in Chapter 9, we can foster deep connections with young people and sustain those connections.

Equip · Inspire · Impact

- Design communications with the recipient in mind.
- Consider how you respond to the good news youth share with you, striving for an active and constructive response.
- Be mindful of when you are at your best communicating and when you struggle to communicate, and schedule important conversations accordingly.

Empathy

"Could a greater miracle take place than for us to look through each other's eye for an instant?"

— *Henry David Thoreau*

Empathy is a tool of compassion, and true empathy means we must be willing to sit with someone in their emotions. It is an important relational skill as it allows us to be in authentic connection with others. Empathy is a notable component of connecting with others in a non-judgmental space.

Empathy has two different forms: cognitive empathy and affective empathy, as theorized by Dr. Theresa Wiseman, a nursing scholar. Cognitive empathy originates from intellectual activities, such as thinking and reasoning, whereas affective empathy stems from feelings and emotions.

Here are the four steps of cognitive empathy:

- **Perspective-taking**: Viewing another's experience through our own lens.
- **Stay out of judgment**: Listening without evaluating the experience.

- **Recognizing others' emotions**: Finding something in ourselves to help us connect with their emotions.
- **Communicating our understanding of emotion**: Expressing acknowledgment of the emotion, such as "That's tough. I see your sadness" or "I see how happy you are."

Affective empathy is experience sharing, a process of attuning one's emotions to another's personal experience. Caution should be exercised with this approach, as it can lead to an undesirable outcome, drawing us into another's emotional state. This is often where compassion fatigue arises. We can be available and supportive in many capacities, but it is unhealthy to take on the issues and emotions of others as our own. Individuals with strong empathic tendencies can fall prey to compassion fatigue.

> Empathy asks us to do nothing, know nothing, and compare to nothing.

Brené Brown does an excellent job comparing empathy to many other emotions:

- **Empathy:** "I get it."
- **Sympathy:** "I feel sorry for you."
- **Judgment:** "Shame on you."
- **Disappointment:** "You've let me down."
- **Advice-giving and problem-solving:** "I can fix this, and I can fix you."

Now, let's take a look at empathy in practice with Dillian. Dillian isn't invited to a party, and Mom could respond in any of the ways mentioned above. She could tell him that she feels sorry for him, showing sympathy by distancing herself from the emotion since she can't relate to it. Judgment was an option, too: "You should have been nicer to them." If she went into problem-solving mode, she'd likely say something like "I can fix this; let me call their mother," which sends the message "You aren't capable. I can fix this because you can't." But fortunately, Mom chose empathy by saying, "I get it. It's hard being excluded." Mom nailed it!

When we respond with empathy, we hold space for another person to process their emotions. It removes the weight of feeling like we need to respond with solutions. Empathy asks us to do nothing, know nothing, and compare to nothing. The only demand empathy places on us is to be present and acknowledge another's emotions.

Equip · Inspire · Impact

- **Model empathy when interacting with youth.**
- **When engaging in empathy, refrain from problem-solving or sharing similar experiences.**
- **Be willing to sit with a young person in their pain without attempting to remove the hurt.**

Resolving Issues

"The time is always right to do what is right."
— *Dr. Martin Luther King, Jr.*

Issues between people are inevitable. They can range from minor concerns to major breakdowns. It takes tremendous courage to approach challenges with others, especially as it is often perceived as confrontational, which is, by definition, a negative and hostile act.

Have you ever wondered why it is easier for young people to talk about someone than to someone? Is it because they don't want to hurt them? Aren't they hurting them by talking about them, allowing the problem to linger, and discussing it with others? As adults, when interacting with youth, our failure to address issues directly with them may result in missed growth opportunities, as we do not provide feedback that could benefit the youth's development and interactions with others.

One method to encourage young people to use when approaching issues between people is to look at the situation from the perspective of time.

Past: It happened. They can't change the past, but they can learn from it.

Present: In the moment is where the ability exists to have a real impact.

Future: Is influenced by their present actions.

Shannon and Cindy's story illustrates this well. Shannon canceled plans at the last minute with Cindy, her best friend since third grade. Shannon is miserable as she not only hurt Cindy, but she also did it to join a more popular group of girls who were mean and talked badly about Cindy the entire evening.

Past: Shannon recognizes her mistake and is appropriately remorseful, but lamenting it won't resolve the problem. She can't quit thinking about what she did, and ruminating about what could have or should have happened is making her feel worse.

Present: Shannon realizes this won't go away on its own and decides to respond quickly. She realizes that the longer this continues, the bigger the problem will grow. She plans her approach using the following prompts:

- **Define the issue:** What specifically is the problem?
  - Action: Shannon is clear; the issue is that she chose others over Cindy and excluded her from the group.
- **Identify fears:** Consider what concerns are affecting your ability to have the conversation.
  - Action: Shannon is embarrassed by her behavior, remorseful for her actions, and afraid Cindy won't forgive her.

- **Construct a message:** Think in advance about what you will say and how you will say it.
  - Action: Shannon carefully considers how she will speak with Cindy.

- **Be honest:** Minimizing an issue rarely helps and often makes it more difficult to get the point across. It can delay progress without ever finding a resolution. When you fail to say what needs to be said, you will inevitably face this conversation again in the future.
  - Action: Shannon decides to be honest and straightforward when she speaks with Cindy.

- **Be goal-oriented:** Decide in advance if the goal is to heal or end this relationship.
  - Action: In this situation, Shannon genuinely wants to mend her relationship with Cindy.

- **Have the conversation:** Reach out and talk to the person directly; avoid discussing the problem with others.
  - Action: Shannon asks Cindy to meet her in person to have the conversation.

- **Lead with the positive:** It can be helpful to share how important the relationship is and be direct about wanting to resolve this.
  - Action: Shannon tells Cindy how she values her and her long-time friendship.

- **Be empathetic:** Recognize how you have felt in similar circumstances and how the other might be feeling.
  - Action: Shannon remembers how hurt she was when she was excluded in the past. She tells Cindy, "I am so sorry for my actions. I know how hurt I would be if you had done this to me."

- **Consider timing and location:** Ensure both parties will be comfortable and that you are not rushed or interrupted.
  - Action: The girls meet after school in the park to talk instead of in the hall between classes. Shannon and Cindy have the conversation. They sit together in discomfort and awkwardness, but they do it and work through it, recognizing that it is acceptable to feel that way.

Future: Shannon and Cindy commit to moving forward, and they do. They just designed their future with an even stronger friendship grounded in empathy.

Another approach for young people to repair a relationship when an action or word has caused harm is to apologize. On some occasions, a simple and sincere "I'm sorry" is sufficient. There are a myriad of ways to apologize effectively. Apologies will be unique to the individual and custom to the situation.

When an occasion requires a more substantial apology, encourage youth to try the template below. Restorative justice practices developed this process for an effective apology.

I accept responsibility for (action)_____.
I recognize my actions of (specific behavior)_____,
    caused (specific problem)_____.
I know that must have made you feel (express empathy)_____.
I am sorry for (specific actions)_____.
I would like to move forward. Are you willing? (this may include
    a request for forgiveness)
The (action or service) I intend to do to make up for this
    is _____.

This formal approach might feel inauthentic for a young person, but remind them it's just a framework. Here is the concept in conversation: "Hey Mom, I'm sorry I didn't do the dishes, and I know that caused more work for you. I really let you down, and you must be super disappointed in me. Can you forgive me? I'll make up for it by doing dishes for the next three days."

Manuel's story is another great example of an effective apology in action. Manuel received a one-day in-school suspension for disrupting his math class. Before class starts the next day, Manuel approaches Mr. Adams with the following apology.

"I accept responsibility for disrupting the class. I recognize that arguing with Noah and throwing a book stopped you from teaching and got the whole class off track. I am disappointed in my actions, which must have made you feel frustrated. I am sorry for arguing with Noah and throwing a book, which caused everything to stop. Would you please accept my apology and allow me to return to class? I would like to make up for this by helping you after school, and I am committed to not doing this again. Would this work for you?"

> A thoughtful restoration process can rebuild and redefine relationships.

Mr. Adams is the recipient of the apology, which he perceives as sincere. He accepts the apology with grace and wisdom, sets boundaries, defines expectations for the future, and moves forward while encouraging Manuel to do the same. He doesn't forget what happened but doesn't dwell on it, bring it up, or judge Manuel. Of course, if the behavior continues, that will need to be addressed.

Resolving issues between yourself and youth is paramount to youth developing these skills. Youth are more likely to be receptive to actively resolving issues when they have been on the receiving end of a caring adult practicing this process. Did you have plans with a young person, but a work meeting ran over? Did you blame them for something that was not their fault after all? How you handle those moments will directly influence their perception of how issues are resolved. Additionally, have conversations with them about how you address issues at work or with friends. When young people bring up their people issues, don't dismiss them as insignificant or solve the issues for them, but help them develop their resolution skills.

Resolving issues requires effort from everyone involved. Missteps and problems are inevitable for young people, but a thoughtful restoration process can rebuild and redefine relationships. Adults who model healthy behaviors and accept sincere apologies with grace can help young people develop strong people skills related to resolving issues.

Equip · Inspire · Impact

- **Provide youth with the framework for an effective apology, and when applicable, assist them in crafting one.**
- **Model effective resolution skills when apologizing to or receiving an apology from young people.**
- **Prioritize healthy relationships and interactions.**

Reconnecting and Disconnecting

"Get past your past, be a presence in your present, and let no one refute your future."
— *Johnnie Dent Jr.*

Relationships consist of the needs, wants, and desires of all parties involved, and it is unrealistic to expect that these components will always align. The complexity of relationships can make them challenging for young people to navigate. Relationships can be healthy or unhealthy, and often, youth do not recognize the difference. It may be assumed that healthy relationships are common and develop naturally, but that's not typically the case.

Sharing with young people what a healthy or unhealthy relationship looks like can help them set realistic expectations and identify potential problems. Healthy relationships share accountability, power, and decision-making, are mutually beneficial, allow for open conversations, feel safe, foster personal growth, and cultivate an environment of honesty and trust. Unhealthy relationships, on the other hand, often include a power imbalance, deception, restriction of one party, isolation, neglect, abuse, and fear, and they favor one party.

Even healthy relationships will likely experience significant challenges at some point. A crucial component of healthy relationships is that both parties work through and resolve challenges together. When they cannot be completely resolved, the parties involved work to manage the challenges effectively. Determining if a relationship is healthy or unhealthy can help inform a young person of the approach they will take when resolving issues.

Years of work, commitment, and trust can be diminished or destroyed in a single act. A scenario with Kennedy shows just how easily this can occur. Kennedy had earned her parents' trust, which they demonstrated by letting her drive the car and stay out late on weekends. They never questioned her when she said she was staying somewhere or doing something. This changed when Kennedy attended a party her parents said she couldn't. Uncharacteristically, she went to the party but told her parents she was staying at a friend's house. All the parents, including Kennedy's, were notified when some of the underage teens were caught drinking.

> A crucial component of healthy relationships is that both parties work through and resolve challenges together.

Kennedy knew she had made a mistake and felt horrible. Her parents were extremely disappointed and felt they could no longer trust her. The next night at dinner, Mom handed Kennedy a piece of paper.

"Crinkle this up as small as you can," Mom said. Kennedy looked apprehensively at Mom and then at Dad. She made the paper into a small ball and held it in her hand.

"Now put it back to what it was a minute ago," directed Mom.

Kennedy stared at the paper and began to unfold it. She laid it on the table and pressed it as flat as she could.

"What's wrong, Kennedy? Is it the same?" asked Dad.

Kennedy focused on the paper, having a good idea of where this was going. "No."

"What happened?" Dad said quietly.

"It's changed," whispered Kennedy.

"Can you still use it?" he asked.

"Yes," Kennedy said, looking at the paper.

"What can you do to return it to the state it was before the occurrence?" Mom inquired.

"Nothing. Nothing at all..." responded Kennedy.

"What are we telling you, Kennedy?" asked Mom.

"Once you do something like I did, you can't undo it." Kennedy cried, "I'm so sorry. I didn't mean to hurt you, and now you will never trust me again."

"We will work through this, and we will trust you again. It may take time," said Dad. "We still believe in you. This was an important lesson, and thankfully, no one got hurt. That being said, once a word has been spoken or an action taken, it cannot be undone. But you can move forward with the lessons learned."

Like Kennedy and her parents, many relationships fluctuate between harmonious, struggling, and damaged, with few perpetually in a state of high cohesion. All relationships require work; some require less work than others.

Youth need skills to intentionally build good relationships. A solid plan for developing and maintaining a good relationship is worth the investment. Here are some thoughts to share with them:

- **Create ground rules.** Define what is acceptable and what isn't. Ensure that both parties' expectations are clearly expressed and understood.
- **Have a communication plan.** This is important in good times and even more so in challenging times. How will

you communicate when one or both of you are not at your best?

- **Have an alternate plan.** Relationships will likely face challenges at some point. It's better to be prepared.

When something goes awry, young people can ask themselves if it's a relationship that should be reconnected or disconnected. Many relationships will need to be healed before they can continue forward. Occasionally, some are better than they were before the mishap if handled well. Others may need separation, as there is little or no hope of moving forward in a healthy manner.

When considering a damaged relationship, it can help youth to begin with the end in mind. The approach will be distinctively different depending on their desired outcome. The best way to reconnect or repair a relationship is not to break it in the first place. As Kennedy demonstrated, relationships rely on trust, and trust is often difficult to regain once it is lost.

When an offense has occurred, forgiveness—a concept many young people are familiar with—has value. There are varying degrees of wronging someone, from forgetting to return a call to causing great bodily harm. There is also a wide range of solutions to issues, from quickly acknowledging and apologizing to completely ending the relationship. For this purpose, we will consider concerns in the mid-range.

In Discover You™, we utilize forgiveness as a tool to help the offended individual move forward, not necessarily as an extension of grace to the offender. In our early days, I coached a group of teenagers in forgiveness. This group consisted of young people who had been wronged in ways difficult for me to imagine, with many actively living in these situations. Some were in negative family dynamics, while others found themselves in unhealthy relationships with peers or romantic partners.

Jessie was one of our participants in Discover You™, who, during a forgiveness activity, crossed her arms, set her jaw, and adamantly declared, "I will never forgive him. He doesn't deserve it." Years ago, Jessie's father abandoned her, her mother, and her sister, leaving them to struggle emotionally and financially. I was at a loss when I attempted to encourage Jessie to see the advantage of forgiveness. From my perspective, Jessie could have benefited from channeling this energy into focusing on her future. I told her as much, and it did not go as I had hoped.

It took some time and deep consideration to uncover a way to convey a healing message, ultimately leading to a shift in our approach. Once identified, the next challenge was sharing that message while equipping deeply hurt individuals.

Forgiveness in this model presents freedom for the individual who was wronged, not the offender. If you hold a different belief, we are not disparaging it; we are simply separating the two actions for the sake of those who are wronged.

We identified an ABC process of **Acknowledge**, set **Boundaries**, and **Choose**:

Acknowledge: Youth name what happened, who did it, why it was wrong, and that they didn't deserve it. Jessie writes, "My father abandoned my mother, sister, and me. It was wrong to leave us like that. We didn't deserve that. He would promise to come visit or send money, but he never did."

Boundaries: Youth set boundaries to ensure it doesn't happen to them again, and if possible, so it can't happen to someone else. Remember, many of these young people are actively living in a nightmare and feel helpless about getting out or changing it. The boundaries Jessie had set years prior were to stop talking to her father when he called and not believe him when he told her mother he was sending money or going to visit her or her sister.

Choose: Youth choose to move forward. They may need to consciously choose 100 times a day, but they still choose. Encourage them to free themselves and embrace their future. Over time, hopefully, the frequency of having to choose will diminish. Jessie wrote, "I choose to no longer let him control my life. Some days, it is easier than others, but whenever I think of him, I tell myself we're better off without him. We didn't deserve it, and we have a great life today and ahead of us."

The challenge for many young people who have been wronged is in telling the offender they "forgive them." Each person needs to decide that for themselves. If their goal is to heal a relationship, they may choose to extend forgiveness to the individual who wronged them. Perhaps that is a choice Jessie eventually made, but she made the most important choice: to recover her own life.

Sometimes, relationships require disconnection, as staying in them can be unhealthy. Those can be difficult choices to make for youth. When young people decide to end an unhealthy relationship, keep a few things to share with them:

- Prioritize yourself as you are responsible for your personal wellbeing.
- Be firm but kind as long as you can be, recognizing there are occasions where you can only be firm.
- Ask others for support; friends and family can often help.
- Try to clearly and consistently communicate your commitment to ending the relationship. Wavering creates confusion and can prolong the process.

- Remove yourself and limit your exposure to the other person as much as possible.
- Get professional help as needed, whether it is a therapist because you need to talk, or legal support if the situation is spiraling out of control.

Disconnection can be exceptionally difficult for our youth. Remember, they often have a limited number of people and experiences, and whichever piece of their life they may be losing could be significant to them. Whenever our youth are struggling with familial relationships, we suggest professional counseling.

Relationships. There are healthy ones and unhealthy ones. There are good days and bad days. They can be repaired, and they can be ended. Young people can choose to adopt a model of forgiveness that sets them free. Forgiveness means different things to different people. When it comes to the young people in our lives, our priority is first them and their ability to function through hurt and difficult relationships. As caring adults, we must remember it is our role to provide tools, not choose for them.

Equip · Inspire · Impact

- **Use a simple piece of paper to demonstrate the importance of thought before action and the fragility of relationships.**
- **Isolate and share the components of forgiveness (Acknowledge, set Boundaries, Choose) to allow young people to move forward.**
- **Encourage professional support for young people, particularly in complex family situations.**

Part III

Purpose. Motivation. Intention.

Purpose. Motivation. Intention.

"We cannot live only for ourselves. A thousand fibers connect us with our fellow men."
— *Herman Melville*

The gym reeked of despair as the student body and staff mourned the loss of yet another young person who had been ripped from this world. Officer Sanchez, North Side High's Student Resource Officer, pivoted between profound grief and uncontrollable rage as he approached the basketball coach, Tom Jenkins.

Coach Tom's gut told him the news would be crushing. He also knew this horrific event would be like the stones he would toss in the pond as a kid. The gradient ripples would be visible for a time, but the disruption under the surface would ensure the pond would never be the same again. Today, a stone hit the pond.

"One dead, one in critical condition," Officer Sanchez said, clearly shaken.

Coach Tom hesitated, as there was no good answer to his next question, "Who?" The information would inform both his and the school's immediate course of action. Coach Tom led the school's Emergency Response Team (ERT). One of the ERT's responsibilities was to aid students and staff in navigating the emotions and challenges surrounding the loss of a fellow staff member or student.

"Eugene Fox is dead. Simone Ortiz is hanging on, barely," he replied.

"Details?" asked Coach Tom.

"We don't know everything yet, other than a group of kids were partying by the river. It sounds like there was a disagreement, and now we have two shooting victims," replied Officer Sanchez.

Days followed, ultimately forcing those left behind to face the aftermath of death. The family, students, and community gathered around the grave of Eugene, one of their own. Each was present for their own reasons. The students mourned their own mortality and the fragility of their lives. Many barely knew Eugene, some not at all. They came to the grave hoping to find the part of themselves they lost and to make sense of the unexplainable. Few found solace.

"Thanks for coming, Coach Tom. It means a lot to my mom. She's really destroyed over this," said Dylan with all the bravado he could muster. The days had been a blur, and it was at the funeral that Coach Tom connected with Dylan, one of Eugene's two younger brothers. Coach Tom extended his hand to shake Dylan's. He accepted it hesitantly, then leaned in for the acceptable handshake embrace, trembling and clearly wrecked.

"Of course. I'm so sorry for your loss and that of your family. I know you and Eugene were close. This must be extremely hard for you," said Coach Tom. "Reach out to me next week, will you? I'd like to help if I can."

"No one can bring Eugene back, can they?" Dylan reflected, knowing and not expecting an answer.

Dylan didn't come to school the week after the funeral, and no one had seen him. Coach Tom had tried to provide space considering the loss, but his concern grew with each passing day. He knew from experience that loss takes its most profound hold after the funeral has ended. Coach Tom knew that Dylan had idolized his older brother Eugene. Eugene had been aware of this and had worked hard to shield Dylan from his use of drugs and involvement in illegal activities. As Eugene's life took an even darker turn, he encouraged Dylan to participate in sports and focus on his studies. While he had given up on himself, Eugene had hoped that Dylan would become the first in their family to go to college and make something of himself.

Coach Tom saw the same possibilities for Dylan and wished to champion Eugene's wishes for his little brother. Instead of waiting for Dylan to reach out or return to school, Coach Tom showed up at Dylan's home. "Hello, Ms. Fox. I'm so sorry for your loss. Is there anything I can do to support you and the boys?" he asked as he noticed shiny floors, vacuumed carpet, and sparse furnishings.

"The help I need is with Dylan, so if you are here to see him, you are a relief," she replied.

Odious music roared from the upstairs room, requiring several loud knocks before Dylan answered the bedroom door.

"I appreciate you showing up, Coach Tom, but there's nothing for you here," said Dylan as he turned away.

"We're missing you at school, Dylan. I think it's important for you to come back."

"Not happening," said Dylan. "None of it matters anyway."

"What are your plans?" prodded Coach Tom.

"Got none. Don't need any," Dylan said.

"What about Jason?" asked Coach Tom regarding Dylan's younger brother.

"He'll be fine. He's got my mom and his friends," he replied.

"Are you sure?"

Over the next hour, Coach Tom asked thoughtful questions, listened attentively, and persuaded Dylan that he mattered and that his life mattered. Now, he was the big brother for Jason to look up to. Eventually, Dylan agreed to return to school the next day and said he would stop by the gym to see Coach Tom. He was true to his word, though he appeared a wisp of his former self in size and demeanor. Coach Tom felt relief that Dylan had simply shown up because it was a first step in what would be a lifelong journey of healing and coping for Dylan.

When Eugene died, Dylan lost his biggest supporter. He also lost his sense of purpose and motivation. What had made sense to him in the past suddenly didn't. He could no longer find meaning in his actions and lacked motivation for anything. He was at war with himself to breathe and move. Dylan was mourning the loss of his loved one and had given up on life itself.

"I'm worried about Jason and my mom," Dylan shared. "They are having a hard time. My whole family is falling apart, and I can't seem to get out of bed or do anything to help."

Coach Tom recognized Dylan's concern for his family as the immediate motivation he needed to find purpose in life again. That day marked the beginning of the path to their family's future as Coach Tom supported Dylan in intentionally and meaningfully moving his family—and, most importantly, himself—toward healing.

Chapter 7

Purpose

"When you walk in purpose, you collide with destiny."
— *Ralph Buchanan*

Purpose is a young person's what. It is an intention to accomplish something meaningful for themselves and the world. When life has purpose, young people have a meaningful and positive aim, and they live with intention. Purpose is the reason something exists.

Meaning is a young person's why. It provides them with the sense that their life matters, and it is how they comprehend the world. When life has meaning, it makes sense; it is valuable and beneficial, and youth are living deliberately.

Understanding purpose and meaning can increase young people's happiness, motivation, commitment, satisfaction, and performance. Finding and leveraging their 'what' and 'why' increases the meaning in their lives. Living with meaning and purpose is a common trait in successful and thriving individuals.

A study I read about meaning and purpose caused me to think differently about some of my ideas surrounding suicide. Far too many young people contemplate, attempt, and succeed at ending their own lives. They are making irrevocable choices in a single moment during a stage in life where they are ill-equipped mentally and emotionally to make such a permanent decision.

In 2014, Shigehiro Oishi, a personality and social psychologist and associate professor at the University of Virginia, partnered with Ed Diener, a leading researcher of positive psychology for the Gallup organization, to conduct a comprehensive study across 132 countries. Their research examined levels of happiness and meaning, along with factors such as wealth and suicide rates.

They found that people in wealthier regions, such as those in Scandinavia, reported being happier than those in poorer regions, like Sub-Saharan Africa. But when it came to meaning, Model living a purposeful and meaningful life. their findings were strikingly different. Wealthy places like France and Hong Kong had some of the lowest levels of meaning. Poor nations, such as Niger and Ethiopia, however, had some of the highest levels of meaning, although they were among the unhappiest in the study. Here's where it gets interesting. Wealthier nations had higher suicide rates than less affluent ones. The study suggested that it was not happiness or unhappiness that predicted suicide, but meaning or lack thereof.

Suicide rates are staggering and are the second leading cause of death for our young people between 10 and 24. Needless to say, we need to work on meaning and purpose. It's about young people understanding their 'why'. This helps them to understand what motivates them and can inspire them to work through adversities and be more resilient. You can encourage young people to explore their meaning and purpose in many ways, reminding them it is a process and a journey, and not to be discouraged if they have yet to discover it. Here are some suggestions you can try:

- Help youth attach to something bigger than themselves, such as a club or a movement.
- Provide them with an important role in the family or community. Meaning and purpose can be more challenging in isolation.
- Inspire a discussion about their unique and meaningful contribution to the whole or larger community.
- Prompt youth to engage with like-minded people.
- Reframe mundane tasks by connecting youth with a higher purpose.
- Encourage youth to serve others through volunteering or mentoring someone with a similar interest.
- Recommend they participate in meet-up groups.
- Have them practice five-minute favors, which means saying yes to requests from others that will take less than five minutes and will not diminish them.
- Suggest they be reflective and mindful as they consider their actions as related to purpose and meaning.
- Explore meaning and purpose with young people using the following prompts:
    ◦ What do you want to do?
    ◦ How do you want to do it?
    ◦ Why do you want to do it?

As you interact with youth, remember that your behavior and actions are more impactful than your words. You are modeling behaviors, be they intentional, healthy, or destructive. Take this opportunity to model living a purposeful and meaningful life. Can you answer the same questions? What do you want to do? How do you want to do it? Why do you want to do it? I expect that many of you live intentionally and find meaning in your work and interactions with young people. I applaud you, as that is, in itself, a meaningful pursuit.

Equip · Inspire · Impact

- Identify your meaning and purpose.
- Assist young people in identifying their meaning and purpose by asking thoughtful questions, such as: What do you want to do? How do you want to do it? Why do you want to do it?
- Provide opportunities for youth to uncover their meaning and purpose through volunteering, joining clubs, and helping others.

Values

"Your beliefs become your thoughts, your thoughts become your words, your words become your actions, your actions become your habits, your habits become your values, your values become your destiny."

— *Gandhi*

Values are the beliefs young people have about what is important. The list of values is endless, and may include concepts such as dignity, honesty, integrity, compassion, or family. Values drive every decision youth make and are a key component in each of the five tenets of social and emotional learning:

- **Self-Awareness:** Understanding one's values becomes critical to increasing self-awareness by understanding oneself and how one interacts with others.
- **Self-Management:** Values assist in self-management because, as youth increase their knowledge of what is important to them, they can make more informed choices about how they present themselves in the world.
- **Social Awareness:** Understanding personal values can help

young people understand how they fit in social situations and what might motivate others.

- **Relationships:** How values manifest in youth behaviors affect their relationships.
- **Responsible Decision-Making:** Values are at the core of influencing decisions.

Brené Brown lists over 100 values in her book, *Dare to Lead*. This broad approach provides opportunities to consider values, and you may have a few to add to the list.

Youth have a multitude of values that arise under different conditions. Many young people can list about five values that are central to their identity. These core values tend to present themselves, invited or not. Often, when triggered, they incite an outward reaction before a young person can give much thought to how they intend to respond.

Here are a few nuances regarding values:

- They are a representation of what is important to youth in life.
- Each young person holds numerous values with varying degrees of importance.
- Values should be seriously considered when making decisions, setting goals, and taking action.
- Values transcend specific actions and situations and are generally consistent.
- A young person's values are prioritized relative to one another. For example, they may value honesty and friendship. When those values become competing in a situation, one must win out or take priority over the other.
- As everyone holds different values, and values compete for priority at any given moment, we should not assume that what we value is what other people should or do value. It

VALUES

- Accountability
- Achievement
- Adaptability
- Adventure
- Altruism
- Ambition
- Authenticity
- Balance
- Beauty
- Being the Best
- Belonging
- Career
- Caring
- Collaboration
- Commitment
- Community
- Compassion
- Competence
- Confidence
- Connection
- Contentment
- Contribution
- Cooperation
- Courage
- Creativity
- Curiosity
- Dignity
- Diversity
- Environment
- Efficiency
- Equality
- Ethics
- Excellence
- Faith
- Family
- Financial Stability
- Forgiveness
- Freedom
- Friendship

- Fun
- Future Generations
- Generosity
- Giving Back
- Grace
- Gratitude
- Growth
- Harmony
- Health
- Home
- Honesty
- Hope
- Humility
- Humor
- Inclusion
- Independence
- Initiative
- Integrity
- Intuition
- Job Security
- Joy
- Justice
- Kindness
- Knowledge
- Leadership
- Learning
- Legacy
- Leisure
- Love
- Loyalty
- Making a Difference
- Nature
- Openness
- Optimism
- Order
- Parenting
- Patience
- Patriotism
- Peace

- Perseverance
- Personal Fulfillment
- Power
- Pride
- Recognition
- Reliability
- Resourcefulness
- Respect
- Responsibility
- Risk Taking
- Safety
- Security
- Self-Discipline
- Self-Expression
- Self-Respect
- Serenity
- Service
- Simplicity
- Spirituality
- Sportsmanship
- Stewardship
- Success
- Teamwork
- Thrift
- Time
- Tradition
- Travel
- Trust
- Truth
- Understanding
- Uniqueness
- Usefulness
- Vision
- Vulnerability
- Wealth
- Wellbeing
- Wholeheartedness
- Wisdom
- _____

↖ Add yours here!

is better for a young person to consider what the other person might value and how a situation might challenge the other's values.

There are many ways to help young people identify their values. Try the following:

- Identify values in others:
  - Suggest they think of someone they admire.
  - Then, consider what values that person exhibits.
  - Assess how those values align with their own.

- Identify values through positive outcomes:
  - Suggest they think of a time when everything was working well, and they were feeling positive.
  - Then, identify the values that were being honored at that moment.

- Identify values through challenging situations:
  - Identify a time when they were facing an internal struggle.
  - Then, discern the values that were being challenged or ignored in that instance.

- Identify values through strong reactions:
  - Name something that incites a strong reaction.
  - Next, identify what values are surfacing in those moments.

When we spend significant time together as a family or group, we can begin to assume that we share the same values and that our priorities are similar to theirs. Remember, values compete for prioritization, so even when we share values, they work in relationship to our other values. For example, teens value friends and family; during adolescence, those two values often cause an internal battle for top place.

Since values create feelings, it makes sense that when values are honored, youth experience positive feelings, and when values are challenged, their feelings become negative. That concept is particularly effective in understanding others. When you witness negative behaviors, you can expect that a value is being threatened. With that understanding, you can help young people explore their attitudes and feelings toward a given situation and use that information to identify what values are being threatened. Then, address accordingly.

Youth are most effective and fulfilled when they are in situations or behaving in manners that align well with their values. Understanding what they value helps them be better humans and better

Youth are most effective and fulfilled when they are in situations or behaving in manners that align well with their values.

versions of themselves. When they are in alignment with their values, they can experience a true sense of belonging. They can feel disconnected when they behave in a manner that does not align with their values.

Consider conflicting values with Arianna and Felipe. They are brother and sister who seem to be in a continual state of battle. One wants to arrive at school at 7:00, the other at 7:15—battle. One wants to go to a theme park for vacation, the other to a national park—battle. One wants to watch a horror show, the other a comedy—battle.

Their aunt Diana is losing her patience while spending the weekend with them. She remembered a values exercise she had done at a Discover You™ training and decided to try it again. Diana handed each of them a list of values and instructed them to work independently to select the top five that represented what was most important to them.

Arianna chose achievement, family, justice, creativity, and passion, while Felipe chose courage, teamwork, honesty, belonging, and resilience.

"What is something you two disagree on?" asked Aunt Diana.

"What time to leave for school," said Felipe, and Arianna agreed.

"Why do each of you choose the time you do?" inquired Aunt Diana.

Felipe responded, "I want to go to school to see my friends and work on projects."

Arianna said, "I want to be home to spend time with Mom before school."

"What value might each other be honoring?" asked Aunt Diana.

"Felipe is probably honoring teamwork or belonging," replied Arianna.

"Arianna is probably honoring family," replied Felipe.

They both agreed.

"How can this help you two understand each other?" asked Diana.

The conversation that followed was more insightful than Diana had expected. Arianna and Felipe realized each other's actions were motivated by things they valued. One conversation didn't resolve all their issues, but it did provide a common language and a starting point for future discussions.

Helping young people recognize and honor their values can provide them with clarity in their lives. The heavy influence that values have on individuals affects their decisions and choices. Understanding what values are threatened can help youth understand why they respond or feel certain ways in various circumstances. Recognizing what others value can help build healthy relationships and provide insight into their actions.

Equip · Inspire · Impact

- Identify your core values and how they are reflected in your daily life.
- Consider a young person who is exhibiting challenging behaviors. What values may they be demonstrating?
- Share a list of values and encourage young people to identify their values and how they affect their lives.

Mindfulness

"Always be on the lookout for the presence of wonder."
— *E.B. White*

Mindfulness is an intentional way of being in the world, paying attention to the details of the present moment, and living in the present. It is the conscious awareness of the present moment, where one intentionally thinks about what is happening to and around oneself. This is the opposite of just passing time or going through the motions of life. Mindfulness optimizes the brain's learning capacity. Focusing on fewer things allows for better concentration on each thing. By realizing when we are splitting our attention in too many directions, learning to prioritize the many tasks we need to accomplish, and focusing on one thing at a time, we likely not only get things done, but they are also done well.

Mindfulness also helps young people improve self-control and self-regulation. When they practice mindfulness, they take control of their mind's direction by choosing what they focus on; it follows that by controlling their focus, they also control themselves. The more youth practice, the more control they have. Resiliency and decision-making are increased through mindfulness because focusing on the present allows youth to make more thoughtful decisions as time is allotted to think things through. Being present in the moment can help youth see problems in the early stages of development, providing the opportunity to avoid them sooner rather than later. Additionally, being aware of others' concerns makes youth less prone to conflict.

> Being present in the moment can help youth see problems in the early stages of development, providing the opportunity to avoid them sooner rather than later.

The best part about mindfulness is that it's accessible and affordable to all of us. Youth simply need to quiet their mind, which can be difficult initially. But mindfulness practice does get easier. Before long, youth are able to allow thoughts to flow in and out without paying undue attention to them.

Encourage young people to take five minutes to practice mindfulness the next time they feel overwhelmed. They can find a comfortable, quiet place to sit where they feel safe. Next, ask them to take several deep breaths and let their eyes close naturally. Then, they should return to a normal breathing rate as they feel the air coming in and out of their body. Encourage them to let thoughts pass through their consciousness without focusing on them. They should continue breathing. Alternatively, they can use a guided meditation, which is available for free on several streaming platforms.

Prompt youth to practice this several times a day, even when things go smoothly. This practice can help make meditation more natural for them and increase the likelihood of using it effectively during times of stress or change. Youth can also use it to shift their attention to a new task or to just settle down after accomplishing something strenuous.

Nicolas provides us with a useful example of mindfulness.

Nicolas struggles with transitions throughout the day and is challenged to focus on classes. He finds himself jumping from one task to the next, often stressed and overwhelmed. His mind races, and he struggles to recall what he has learned.

"You are just not trying hard enough. Nicolas, you need to pay attention," his father expressed with frustration. "We are getting you a tutor, and you better start applying yourself."

Nicolas dreaded working with the tutor because he was convinced he would continue to fail. He tried, but nothing seemed to help, and he wasn't confident that a tutor would change anything. Then, his parents would have an extra reason to be unhappy, spending money only for him to fail again.

The first session with Chris, the tutor, went better than expected, but studying wasn't the only solution. Chris was not a mental health specialist or trained to diagnose learning disorders, which require a specialized approach. However, Chris observed Nicolas's struggles and thought his actual struggle might be with focus. Chris had an idea and hoped Nicholas would go for it.

"Pause, listen, breathe," Chris coached while Nicolas looked at him skeptically.

"My breathing is fine. It's my mind that is struggling," Nicolas replied.

Chris laughed. "Trust me, will you?" Chris explained that he thought Nicolas was challenged by having his mind in too many places at once. He shared the science and history of mindfulness and meditation, explaining why he believed it would be beneficial.

Nicolas agreed to try it for the next few days. Nicolas focused on his breathing and a single thought to signal the transition to the next class. He started to feel more grounded. As he moved through his daily schedule, he leveraged the mindfulness routine that Chris taught him. Gradually, with practice, Nicolas's focus increased, and his stress levels began to drop. Mindfulness became a tool Nicolas used regularly. As a result, his grades improved.

As Nicolas discovered, it takes practice to make this effective. Frequently repeating "pause, listen, breathe" when not stressed creates a habit, so when stressed, the reaction is automatic, allowing you to maintain control. The more you use it in stressful situations, the more effective it will be for you.

Encourage young people to increase their mindfulness by leveraging **breathing**, **senses**, **attitude**, and **actions**. Using Nicolas as an example, we will explore each category.

Breathing: In addition to using mindfulness to manage class transitions, Nicolas found he could employ breathing to control his nervousness before a test. The breathing strategy even worked for him when he found himself getting frustrated or angry. He takes a break and breathes before saying something that might worsen the situation. Even when everything seems to be okay, Nicolas uses breathwork as a relaxation and calming tool.

Senses: Nicolas uses his senses to be more mindful when he goes for walks. This helps him appreciate and enjoy his surroundings more while calming himself. Nicolas enjoys the sounds of the birds chirping and the breeze against his skin. He considers his sense of taste to slow down his eating and take pleasure in his food. Nicolas engages his sense of mindful hearing by listening to music. This helps him release the stresses of the day.

Attitude: Nicolas is mindful of his attitude. He recognizes that optimism helps him to be more hopeful, influencing his decisions and actions. When Nicolas uses this perspective, he finds himself to be more understanding, a better communicator, and a more efficient problem solver. When he is mindful of being grateful for his experiences, he can purposely create the kind of experiences that bring him happiness.

Action: Nicolas has found that expressing gratitude to others increases happiness for both him and the recipient. He notices this positively influences how they interact. He also feels that the little things he does to help others contribute to creating the environment he wants.

The practice of mindfulness can benefit youth by generating increased success and higher-quality decisions, improved focus and clarity, lower stress, and the increased ability to appreciate and savor life's moments. Mindfulness and breathing exercises provide a sense of calm and balance, making the youth's reactions to and management of daily challenges more effective.

Equip · Inspire · Impact

- **Practice mindfulness by incorporating breathing exercises into your daily routine and during times of stress.**
- **Encourage young people to practice mindfulness using controlled breathing when encountering transitions.**
- **Assist youth in increasing their mindfulness by utilizing breathing, senses, attitude, and actions.**

Curiosity and Imagination

"The best use of imagination is creativity. The worst use of imagination is anxiety."

— *Deepak Chopra*

Curiosity is a deep desire to acquire knowledge. It is characterized by inquisitive thinking and the active seeking of information. Curiosity is an innate need to know or explore, fueling a desire to learn, and is often described as a novelty-seeking trait and an openness to new experiences. To wonder is to be curious, which includes a state of amazement and awe. It is learning for the passion of knowing, not for passing a test or meeting the expectations of others. Curiosity could be likened to interest with emotion and is considered a behavior, a characteristic, and an emotion.

As youth develop curiosity, the world becomes more intriguing. Adults who impact youth can engage curiosity to build healthy relationships and encourage youth to explore and expand. The opportunity to sincerely converse occurs when asking curious questions such as "How did you build that model?" or "Tell me what you like about dance." This approach builds relationships while recognizing youth as subject experts who, like us, deepen their curiosity by sharing it with others.

We truly do not discuss or leverage curiosity nearly enough. When youth are curious, they are intrinsically motivated, becoming fueled by the internal desire to discover something of interest to them. When curiosity is sparked in youth, they want to learn and explore, thus propelling themselves forward. Curiosity, like many positive traits and attributes, is innate in varying degrees and, fortunately, can be further developed. Sadly, curiosity can be overlooked in traditional education or undervalued in society, thereby diminishing this valuable skill. Thus, reemphasizing and reinvigorating this attribute may be needed.

Curiosity can be leveraged to open portals to many worlds. It is the driving force behind learning and discovery, acting as a conduit to solutions. Albert Einstein said, "I have no special talent. I am only passionately curious." Einstein's curiosity revolutionized the way the world was understood. Curiosity spurs innovation and invention. One must first be curious or wonder about something with questions such as, "I wonder if there is a more sustainable fuel... I wonder how much water is in a swimming pool... I wonder what my pet is trying to tell me..."

Curiosity is about learning, growing, and exploring. Other benefits of curiosity for our young people include:

- acting as a valuable replacement for judgment or blame by being curious as to why others might think or feel the way they do.
- assisting in resolving disputes because curiosity motivates youth to consider what is concerning or motivating others, and what might be behind a position others hold.
- helping to deconstruct biases and assumptions by being curious about their source and challenging their value.
- increasing mindfulness and awe by inspiring youth to be mindful of the present.

- providing perspective and a broadening worldview as youth gain knowledge.
- combating social anxiety by being prepared with curious questions that enhance conversations.

Relationally speaking, curiosity is a powerful way to connect with others. When youth are genuinely curious, they are more open and inquisitive to others' perspectives and experiences. A curious young person is a good conversationalist who tends to speak less about themselves and encourages others to share more.

Here are some strong, curious questions and prompting statements from our staff that you can leverage with youth:

- **Intended to create awareness:** "Tell me what you think about the homeless people in our community."
- **Challenge possibilities:** "What are some additional options you can come up with?"
- **Open-minded:** "Can you share more with me about that? I had not considered that approach before."
- **Open-ended:** (requiring a response saying more than just yes or no) "Share with me something good that happened in school today." versus "Did you like school today?"
- **Ask what, not why:** (what is curious; why can feel accusatory) "Tell me what you like about soccer." versus "Why do you like soccer?"
- **Genuinely curious:** "I really would like to hear more about this."
- **Explores possible outcomes:** "What do you think will happen if you make that choice?"
- **Not leading and prosecuting:** (framing the question to infer the preferred answer) "You don't want that last piece of cake, do you?" versus "Would you like a piece of cake?"

Questions that spark curiosity foster a sense of belonging and connection, enabling us to explore our differences. They create opportunities to share and learn about one another.

Imagination is a natural result of curiosity. It is the act of creating something new that did not previously exist. Combined with curiosity and hope (Chapter 1), imagination becomes a powerful tool. It combines the possibilities derived from being curious about what could be, with the ability to create something that does not exist, and a vision for the future supported by pathways to achieve that vision.

Elijah possesses the innate traits of curiosity, imagination, and hope. Elijah is six years old and asks more questions than his teachers and parents can answer. He is curious about insects, the weather, and his food source. Where do chicken nuggets come from? How old is the sky? How do antlions design their traps, and why do the ants keep falling in them? He also has a great imagination. He protects dragons by building faraway fortresses. Elijah is hopeful for the world as his path to peace is growing dragon fodder, providing the dragons with a sustainable vegetarian lifestyle, and enabling them to live in harmony with others.

We can learn from Elijah and build imagination in our world using play, exploration, and storytelling. Play is beneficial and applicable to all ages. When youth construct a fort of blankets and chairs, they imagine a world of their own making. When they create crafts, they envision a finished project and then bring that vision to life with their hands. I am an avid crafter and find great joy in doing crafts with young people. I prefer doing organic crafts with them that are open-ended and require imagination, rather than purchased kits that show the end result and all the steps to achieve it. This creates an opportunity for youth to engage their imagination at a deeper level.

Consider the imagination it takes to "build an airplane." Left to their own devices, youth must imagine the plane, see it flying or awaiting a crew on the tarmac, picture its color, wing design, and engine configuration. They must imagine what materials they will build it out of and where they might acquire those materials. They will need to cut, glue, and tweak. Some of them will then add paint to match what they imagined. They can imagine solutions and outcomes when things don't work out as planned. The simple act of building a plane brought imagination to life.

Regardless of age, the process works. If they are two years old, it is a simple plane compared to what they might construct at age 15. Exploration is available to us all, and we must encourage youth to be curious, explore, discover, investigate, and study.

> Encourage youth to be curious, explore, discover, investigate, and study.

The quest itself can be viewed as a playing field for young people's imagination. We can encourage them to explore their home, items in their home, their yard, a park, their city, and the world. For instance, in a wooded area, have them choose a path and encourage the young person to imagine what lies beyond the turn, who built the path, and why. What animals might walk the path? Could there have been prehistoric animals in the park? What games might they play on this path?

Another effective way to strengthen imagination is through storytelling. Storytelling is the ultimate use of imagination, whether the youth are reading a story or telling the story. To our toddlers, you might read a book and ask them to imagine what will happen next or what other color the dog might be. For our elementary and older youth, you could encourage them to imagine how they might end the story or what adventure the lead character might encounter next. Once able to talk, our youth can share the stories of their imagination.

Cultivating imagination is something youth can do wherever they are. Imagination can be best nurtured in an environment where imagination is safe. Within The ROCK, we have intentionally crafted such environments with an imaginative staff. Together, we have been able to imagine a world that does not yet exist, pursue solutions that have not yet been found, and be confident in asking questions such as "What if?"

The wonderful news is that you, too, can be the heroic adult who inspires curiosity and imagination like Elijah's, not the one who diminishes it. We must not stifle or discourage imagination, especially in an attempt to build a serious and thoughtful generation. Suppressing imagination will yield individuals who lack the ability to dream big and the innovative thinking required to solve complex problems. The imaginative Elijahs of this generation and those to follow will become our great thought leaders. Their ability to think extraordinarily and solve new world problems is tied to the imagination and exploration they are showcasing now.

Equip · Inspire · Impact

- **Inspire curiosity when exploring something new, using phrases like "I wonder what would happen if…" or "Might that be possible…?"**
- **Teach youth to use curious questions to increase their ease in social situations.**
- **Invoke imagination through organic crafts and play.**

Kindness

"In a world where you can be anything, be kind."
— *Clare Pooley*

To be kind is to be friendly, compassionate, and considerate. Be kind. I saw a sign in a restaurant that read:

"Be kind to our staff, they are doing their best.
We know you worked all day and are tired, so are we. Our kids are sick too.
We are paying more for everything, too. We just have to make a living, too.
We are understaffed, but we're still here to prepare and serve you the best possible dinner.
Thank you for your kindness – we will be kind to you too."

When did we become a world that had to tell people to be kind? Sure, we did in kindergarten and elementary school, but then we stopped teaching kindness, and some people stopped being kind. There is one resounding message for our youth: be kind.

Kind can look different under different circumstances; you can be kind and assume positive intentions. Most people are genuinely doing the best they can. Being kind is being kind. Not being kind, however, is not the same as being mean. Most people aren't actively mean. But that doesn't mean they are kind. We can be unkind through indifference. Indifference is not kindness. I don't think too many people get out of bed thinking, "I will be mean today," but many people get out of bed and are not kind.

In the bestseller *All I Really Need to Know I Learned in Kindergarten* by Robert Fulghum, a good share of his narrative was around components of kindness:

- Share everything.
- Play fair.
- Don't hit people.
- Put things back where you found them.
- Clean up your own mess.
- Don't take things that aren't yours.
- Say you're sorry when you hurt somebody.

He adds more, including washing your hands and always flushing, which are acts of kindness in their own right that I thought were worthy of mentioning.

Bullying is overt unkindness, which continues to be a problem and affects everyone in its path. Bullying is repetitive aggressive behavior that is uninvited, where a power imbalance is present. Imbalances of power could be physical strength, access to embarrassing information, or popularity that are used to control someone else. Bullying can manifest itself in actions such as making threats, spreading rumors, attacking someone physically or verbally, and excluding someone from a group on purpose. Cyberbullying, developed in conjunction with technology, seemingly doesn't end.

Adults should never tolerate bullying or unkind behaviors. However, stopping inappropriate behavior through our proper and immediate response does not and will not entirely solve the problem. One reason is that you can never "protect" someone else enough. You can't be there at 3 a.m. when an antagonizing text is received or a post is seen on social media; you can't always be in every place. Even if you could stop every incident, the solution is in prevention for both the youth being bullied and the one doing the bullying.

For the youth being bullied, provide them with tools to develop the skills to defend themselves and withstand the behaviors. That sounds counterintuitive. However, youth will encounter bullies their entire lives, and they need to possess the resolve not to let those behaviors destroy them. Discover You™ focuses on cultivating fortitude in young people. Essential tools to equip those affected by bullies are reflected throughout this book, including resilience in Chapter 3, relationship skills in Chapters 4 and 6, social awareness and courage in Chapter 4, and self-worth in Chapter 9.

The bully must first be stopped. Once stopped, Discover You™ focuses on fostering the development of responsible decision-making and prosocial behavior in youth. This book reflects various skills that can help adults teach better behaviors to those who bully, including social awareness in Chapter 4, compassion in Chapter 6, and self-management and self-worth in Chapter 9.

At The ROCK, our staff faced a challenge with Tanya, an eighth-grader who was bullying Hannah, also an eighth-grader. During the school day, Tanya would seek out opportunities to publicly taunt Hannah by calling her names, pushing her, and spreading negative rumors about her. Tanya was repeatedly corrected by adults, but she continued her behavior.

Hannah, who had been attending The ROCK OST program, had begun to miss the program and was withdrawing. When Tanya also decided to join the OST program, Hannah shared with The ROCK staff what was going on at school. The ROCK staff assured Hannah they would be vigilant. Our staff immediately witnessed

Tanya intentionally running into Hannah and then running off laughing.

Though one incident isn't necessarily bullying, the staff addressed the issue immediately with Tanya because they were aware of the previous events. Tanya assured them this was an accident, there were no problems between her and Hannah, and it wouldn't happen again. This was an anticipated response, and bear in mind, these are complex situations where it is impossible to have all the facts.

Due to the history of these two girls, the staff proceeded to define expectations of appropriate behavior. The second time Tanya bullied Hannah in The ROCK program, Tanya's parents were brought in. Though the parents were aware of and frustrated with her behavior, they didn't present a solution. The collective decision was made to remove Tanya from the program for a week. During that time, she would create a plan for how she would behave and share it with the staff and Hannah's parents before returning.

Help our youth develop skills to be self-sufficient, caring, and kind.

A week later, a meeting was held. Tanya shared how she would behave going forward and apologized to Hannah. It was agreed that she could return to the program. How long she stayed was conditional on how she treated others. For a few weeks, things went better. Although Hannah and Tanya weren't friends, they coexisted by staying away from each other. It wasn't ideal, but tolerable. Hannah was again hopeful and able to enjoy the program.

Tanya decided she did not want to get caught bullying again, so she employed new tactics. Outside of The ROCK program, Tanya began quietly encouraging others to terrorize Hannah and found ways to exclude Hannah from everything. When she sent Hannah texts, she used an app designed to delete the message once it was read, making the bullying hard to identify and address.

The ROCK staff offered both families one-on-one Discover You™ coaching for the girls. This consists of a weekly meeting designed in a workshop format. It was offered to Hannah to help her increase her skills in resilience, self-worth, relationship skills, social awareness, and courage. To Tanya, it was offered to help her develop skills of self-management, self-worth, compassion, and social awareness. Both families accepted the support; Hannah continued at The ROCK OST program. Tanya was removed from the program while she worked on herself. We referred both families to counseling with our local youth mental health organization. Again, thankfully, they chose to do that. As adults working to impact youth, we can only provide tools to build skills, and it is important to refer to professionals as needed.

To say "be kind" can feel trivial, especially in circumstances like this. We were fortunate that Tanya's family shared the concern and were supportive. When that is not the case, these situations are even more difficult. After getting support from family and professionals, Tanya grew to understand herself better, became more respectful of others, and learned to control her bullying behaviors. Hannah worked on herself to regain her confidence. Tanya and Hannah never became friends, although they learned to be civil.

As you work with youth, continue to provide them with the necessary tools and engage in meaningful conversations. The goal is to help our youth develop skills to be self-sufficient, caring, and kind. Had Hannah and Tanya received preventative skills training, the situation may have been averted or perhaps more easily resolved. If you are already providing basic tier-one skill-building programs to all youth in your space, kudos to you and your team. If not, consider it an option that will provide a common language and foundational skills to all. Youth are fortunate when caring adults model prosocial behaviors while working to foster foundational skills in them.

Equip · Inspire · Impact

- **Ensure youth understand the components of kindness and that acts of exclusion and indifference are not kindness.**
- **Never tolerate unkind and bullying behaviors.**
- **Incorporate skill-building programs for youth to ensure a solid foundation of respect, teamwork, and expectations.**

Chapter 8

Motivation

"Just do it."

— Nike

Motivation is a component of the self-determination theory, which states that motivation is derived from intrinsic (internal) or extrinsic (external) sources.

The concept of intrinsic motivation helped inspire the Discover You™ program. The thought was to help youth develop and leverage their personal or intrinsic motivation to succeed. The question became: how do you do that?

As caring adults, it is certainly our responsibility to serve as an extrinsic motivational force. However, there is a balance between being that external motivating force and encouraging our youth to become intrinsically motivated. This process requires an awareness of maturity, timing, and thoughtfulness about when extrinsic motivation is appropriate.

To be extrinsically motivated, or motivated by external sources, can be demonstrated with the allegory of the farmer engaging a carrot and a stick to motivate his mule. The carrot is a positive external motivator, acting as a force that encourages or nudges us forward by providing a reward. The stick is a negative external motivator, acting as a force that pushes us away from punishment. Both are outside forces coercing us to behave in a manner preferred by the holder of the carrot and the stick. Both are external pressures to accomplish a goal set by another. One great flaw in the external motivation plan is that as soon as that carrot or stick is removed, so is the motivation. Thus, results are dependent on the continued external force.

Some examples of extrinsic motivation include:

- Reward systems: Do your chores and get a star. How old are youth when they figure out that star holds no real value? Once the perceived value is lost, so is the motivation.
- Grade systems: Do your homework and study, and you'll get a good grade. Good grades equal others' approval, which is only valuable when that approval holds value.
- Opinions of others: People will like you if you behave in a certain way. That idea can be beneficial on occasions such as when the approval reinforces positive and prosocial values. If not, we see negative peer pressure at its finest.

Extrinsic motivation requires an external presence and substantial effort on the part of someone else. Some people view external motivators as superficial, while others are highly motivated by external forces. For many, it depends on the circumstances, who is doing the motivating, and what the motivation is. Positive external motivators include words of affirmation, applause, increased wages, and additional freedoms, all of which are beneficial.

Intrinsic motivation, on the other hand, originates from within the individual. We are compelled to pursue what we desire and value the task or opportunity for its own sake.

Examples of intrinsic motivation include:

- Reading about the solar system because you're genuinely curious.
- Playing on the basketball team because you love the game.
- Studying because you want to do well.
- Scrapbooking because it sparks your creativity.

Intrinsic motivation is more sustainable and is the key to achieving long-term success. We cannot and should not be the ongoing external motivation for success in our youth. If they want to join a team, they will work hard. They will do the work if they want to go to university or trade school. We must, however, play an active and ongoing role in their lives as coaches, mentors, and guides. The concept of intrinsic motivation does not absolve us of our responsibility to support youth in making the best, most informed decisions possible.

When the extrinsic force is no longer available or effective, youth must rely on their intrinsic motivation to keep them on a prosocial and personally productive course. Another consideration is that as youth enter adolescence, their peers gain influence, while the influence of caring adults may wane. Thus, when the youth possess strong intrinsic motivators, they can outweigh or balance what may be negative motivators from their peers.

Consider how self-determination theory causes an interplay between the extrinsic forces acting on a person, the intrinsic motives, and the needs inherent in human nature. This relates to how young people might be affected by autonomy, competence, and relatedness when it comes to being internally or externally motivated. When situations or individuals force youth into something (taking away their autonomy), making them feel incompetent (they are too young to know what they are doing or how to choose), or challenging their ability to relate to others (affecting relationships with peers), they are being motivated by external forces and losing their sense of being in control of their lives.

Motivation is fostered by **Autonomy**, **Competence**, and **Relatedness**.

- **Autonomy:** The right to self-govern and to have a feeling of choice.
- **Competence:** The experience of mastery and effectiveness.
- **Relatedness:** The need to be connected and have a sense of belonging with others.

Holding our youth accountable for their actions is a foundational adult responsibility. Developing an understanding that youth may be free to choose but are not free from the consequences of that choice will help encourage a culture of accountability. This leads us to how discipline and punishment relate to intrinsic or extrinsic motivation.

Punishment is an external force, whereas discipline often originates from an external source but relies on the individual to make choices intrinsically. Punishment states, "As long as I catch you and can inflict pain or loss on you, you will follow my rules and do it my way." Discipline says, "Now that you have knowledge and understanding, you will make appropriate choices for yourself."

At Discover You™, we created the Positive Alternative to School Suspension program, which leverages the lost time of school suspension by helping students build skills and self-awareness, allowing them to return to school more prepared to succeed. In my mind, this was both brilliant and long overdue. To my surprise, I had adults challenging the program because they wanted students punished. They were concerned that students might not see this as punishment and might even enjoy it. It required educating and challenging adults to understand both the short-term and long-term benefits.

Take vaping, for example. Hunter was caught vaping and was punished by receiving an in-school suspension. Hunter disliked being told what to do and having his freedoms removed. Though he continued to vape, he made a conscious choice not to get caught vaping again. Punishment, delivered in various forms, will undoubtedly be effective in causing some youth to change their behaviors; many will simply become better at avoiding detection. Thus, they only change behavior when an external threat exists.

Consider Patrice, who was caught vaping and was disciplined. While being held accountable, she was informed of the health risks of vaping and participated in an exercise where she envisioned her desired future, including

Developing an understanding that youth may be free to choose but are not free from the consequences of that choice will help encourage a culture of accountability.

hiking in Yellowstone National Park. She determined that vaping did not serve her or her goals and chose to stop. This may not work for some, and they will continue vaping, but Patrice and students like her, who choose for themselves that vaping is not a good option, will not vape whether or not someone is watching.

Discipline can help create well-adjusted adults who are capable of responsible decision-making. In the example of Hunter and Patrice, Patrice found intrinsic motivation to make a positive personal choice. Hunter, who did not discover intrinsic motivation, continued the less healthy behavior and focused his motivation on avoiding external punishment.

Punishment, which is extrinsic motivation, only works when the punisher or punishment is a sufficient threat to the individual. Punishment is not a wrong choice and, on occasion, is necessary. Discipline works as a form of personal choice, leveraging gained knowledge, weighing consequences, and creating long-term benefits. Sometimes, both intrinsic and extrinsic motivation are used when punishment is paired with discipline. There is no one path, and you are best positioned to make the decisions for your youth.

How do you achieve the balance between punishment and discipline? How do you assist youth in becoming intrinsically motivated with an internal compass that points in a positive direction? There are various tactics you can use to boost intrinsic motivation. Let's explore how to leverage a few of the skills discussed in this book.

Thought reframing, as discussed in Chapter 1, is an option. In that section, we examined the difference in viewing tasks through the lens of "have to" or "want to." When we say we "have to" do something, it is an external force motivating us. When we encourage our youth to reflect on why something matters to them, they can flip the narrative to "want to," now providing their own motivation.

In Chapter 5, we looked at SMART Plus goals as a means to help achieve personal success. This will also help here. One of the key areas in the Plus section was motivation. Motivation is personal; it is internally or intrinsically driven. Heather's motivation was to graduate from her parents' alma mater and provide her children with a fulfilling childhood.

Living one's purpose and values, as considered in Chapter 7, is another way for our youth to ensure they are motivating themselves. Encouraging youth to understand, explore, and lead with their values will help them prioritize and make choices based on their motivation.

This section explored three concepts: autonomy, competence, and relatedness; intrinsic and extrinsic motivation; and discipline and punishment. We also discovered that motivation is supported by a variety of other skills, traits, and knowledge covered throughout this book. To summarize, as adults, we have an active role in fostering motivation in young people. We share the collective goal of helping youth become prosocial, independent, self-governing, and intrinsically motivated adults.

Equip · Inspire · Impact

- **Seek opportunities to move youth interactions from extrinsic to intrinsic motivation.**
- **Develop a culture and expectation of accountability.**
- **Include skill-building when addressing behavior issues.**

Metacognition and Change

"The price of anything is the amount
of life you exchange for it."
— *Henry David Thoreau*

Metacognition is essentially thinking about thinking. When young people become aware of their thoughts, thinking about what they are thinking can help them analyze those thoughts and determine if they are beneficial. The social-emotional aspects of self-awareness and self-management develop concurrently with metacognition skills. That happens because there is a correlation between youth understanding their thought process and what they are thinking, and increasing self-awareness. That is then followed immediately by thought regulation, which directly supports self-management.

In his book *Metacognition*, James Daniel, a multidisciplinary scholar and author, identifies three types of metacognition: knowledge, regulation, and experience. Collectively, these three types of metacognition identify how individuals understand and perceive their thoughts, thought processes, and related sensations surrounding thinking. Understanding metacognition is the beginning of gaining knowledge and learning how to learn. When young people better understand their thought processes, they become more equipped to self-guide their learning and be intentional with life choices. Similar to a young person requiring a growth mindset to be able to maximize learning and growth, is the need to be an aware thinker. As youth understand the amount of control and influence they have on their lives and outcomes, they become stronger, more confident, and more motivated.

Consider Sheldon's story to gain a better understanding of this theory in practice. Sheldon completed an assignment on clean water in underdeveloped countries, a topic they hoped to pursue in their post-secondary education. They felt they were a fairly serious student but wanted to improve their skills, so they approached Ms. Lambough, their science teacher, and asked for help finding ways to study more effectively. This question was the dream inquiry of most teachers, so she didn't laugh, as they'd warned her not to do, but smiled and jumped in. "I would love to, Sheldon. The best part of learning is understanding how to learn and think," she replied, wondering why we don't teach this to everyone.

"James Daniel recently published a book on metacognition with a concept for learning and problem-solving, which I think you will find interesting." She shared with Sheldon the four steps outlined in *Metacognition*:

- **Planning:** Developing a plan or strategy for approaching a task or problem.
- **Monitoring:** Paying attention to our own thoughts and actions during the learning or problem-solving process.
- **Evaluating:** Assessing our own performance and understanding the task or the problem.
- **Revising:** Adjusting our approach or strategy based on the results of our monitoring and evaluation.

Sheldon and Ms. Lambough captured each of the four steps, and Sheldon immediately began developing the plan. They created a schedule to ensure timeliness and complete the project by the deadline, compiled a list of potential resources, and began drafting an outline for the actual paper. Sheldon thanked Ms. Lambough and headed for the library to begin their research. Throughout the following week, Sheldon monitored their thoughts and how they approached the assignment. They evaluated their performance and realized they studied better when they took a break between the end of the school day and the beginning of their work. A snack helped, too. Sheldon then adjusted their schedule to study when they were most engaged.

> When young people better understand their thought processes, they become more equipped to self-guide their learning and be intentional with life choices.

Ms. Lambough and Sheldon checked in after the first week when Sheldon shared their findings. They were both pleased with the outcomes and increased awareness. Sheldon made a few more adjustments and completed their assignment on time to their and the teacher's satisfaction. Importantly, Sheldon gained a tool that will help them through their academic and professional life. Additionally, Ms. Lambough was inspired to share this practice with all her students.

Being aware of how we think is complemented by understanding change. Change requires motivation and is often more easily managed when one is aware of the stages of the change process. Generally, we don't jump out of bed one morning and decide we need to change something. The moment we decide to make a change is preceded by two stages. There are five total stages of change: **Precontemplation, Contemplation, Preparation/Determination, Action/Willpower,** and **Maintenance.**

Stage One - Precontemplation: The individual does not perceive the need for change, so they are not motivated to make a change.

Examining the struggles Leo faced provides an example. Leo experienced a severe knee injury while playing junior varsity football in ninth grade. This injury involved surgery, extensive healing, and pain medication. Leo's knee improved in good time, rarely giving him pain. However, Leo's misuse of pain medication and substances is escalating. His coach and his father recognize the signs of substance misuse and are prompting Leo to change. However, Leo is in the precontemplation stage and does not think he has a problem.

Stage Two - Contemplation: An individual is considering change.

Leo's substance misuse is creating performance and behavior problems. He is cut from the football team, and his girlfriend ends their relationship. Leo is entering the contemplation stage as he begins to acknowledge that he might need to do things differently.

Stage Three - Preparation/Determination: The person recognizes the need for change and commits to making the necessary adjustments.

A school suspension, the loss of his girlfriend, and the loss of his driving privileges edge Leo into the stage of preparation. He is convinced he needs to change his life and mentally commits to doing so.

Stage Four - Action/Willpower: An individual takes the necessary steps to actively change.

Leo seeks help from a local substance misuse recovery center and begins counseling. He is in the action and willpower stage and is engaging in both. He is no longer misusing substances and is working to stay that way.

Stage Five - Maintenance: The change has been made, and the individual is committed to maintaining the desired behavior and avoiding a return to the previous behaviors that necessitated the change in the first place.

Successfully abstaining from substance misuse, Leo is now in the maintenance stage. He recognizes he needs to take measures to maintain his success and continues in counseling. When he becomes eligible, he begins mentoring others at the recovery center.

Recognizing the five stages of change can help us understand why young people may not be quick to act on the changes you suggest for them. Youth require autonomy to make their own choices and often will not change until they see the need to do so themselves. Leo could not be forced to change, nor could he be inspired to change by others telling him he was headed down the wrong path; he had to experience life's consequences to reach the point where change was his choice, and then he took action to seek it out. The adults in Leo's life also had to understand that change is preceded by the often difficult task of allowing the consequences of life to affect those struggling. It can be hard to stand back and watch young people suffer because of their actions, but it can be important in inspiring change and growth.

Metacognition, or thinking about thinking, can be a pivotal concept for young people as they develop their understanding of the degree to which they influence the outcomes of their lives. Many components of life are beyond a young person's control, but purposefully considering their thoughts and the interplay of those thoughts in their lives is within their control. Additionally, consciously choosing change and recognizing the stages where they or someone they care about may be in the process of change can also provide a greater sense of control over one's life.

Equip · Inspire · Impact

- **Implement Daniel's metacognition concept for learning and problem-solving with youth, including planning, monitoring, evaluating, and revising.**
- **Use the language of the five stages of change when youth are in a transitional period.**
- **Encourage young people to think about how they can manage their thoughts to serve them better.**

Engagement

"Engagement is being one with the music."
— *Martin Seligman*

In terms of positive psychology, engagement describes a specific way of being involved with a task. Engagement is more than being focused; it is about being fully present, showcasing varying levels of interest and concentration. Engagement is one of the six pillars of the science of wellbeing, which we explore in the Evidence-Based Framework section. Engagement reflects the degree of participation young people have in their lives, ranging from minimal to highly engaged.

An interesting and important level of engagement is flow. Flow occurs when we're so absorbed in an experience that we can lose track of time, attending to our basic needs, or the environment around us. Flow is enticing, absorbing, fulfilling, and the state of being highly engaged. For many, it is also productive. But what about when flow isn't as productive or even healthy? Movies, videos, and games can put young people in flow, but these things can become addictive and unhealthy. We will explore ways to help our young people become more engaged in a healthier manner.

Some components of high engagement include challenging

tasks, clear goals, immediate feedback, a sense of control, clear rules, immediate rewards, a visible end, and a deadline. These are some of the key concepts that also make sports and games fun. By applying the construct of engagement, you can create opportunities to help young people enhance their involvement and satisfaction in various areas of their lives.

When formulating the level of challenge for youth, here are some considerations:

- Youth can move from apathy to worry to anxiety when skills are low and the challenge increases.
- Youth can move from apathy to indifference to boredom when the challenge is low and the skill level increases.
- Youth interest increases, and they move toward a state of high engagement when both challenge and skills increase.

There are many ways to encourage young people to increase the levels of engagement in their lives and do so in environments that are beneficial and healthy:

- **Practice mindfulness:** Take time to be present in the moment when experiencing common or new and unique things.
- **Practice savoring:** Experience the food they eat more deeply or enjoy a moment of pleasure.
- **Master a skill:** Develop increased skill levels to draw them into higher challenges.
- **Leverage character strengths:** Use character strengths as explored in Chapter 2.
- **Do things they love:** Participate in what they love and have a passion for.
- **Be in nature:** Engage with nature daily.

CULTIVATING HIGHLY-ENGAGED YOUTH

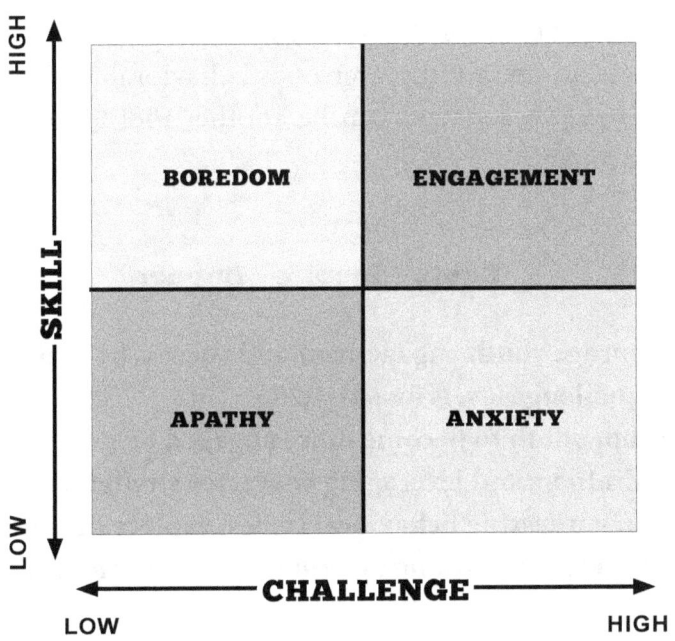

Engagement, like the other pillars of wellbeing, can improve life satisfaction and outcomes. Keep the goal of high engagement in mind when assigning tasks and planning activities. Consider

> Keep the goal of high engagement in mind when assigning tasks and planning activities.

how the skill and/or challenge level could be adjusted to allow youth to be more engaged and achieve greater success. When you witness anxiety, consider whether the skills need to be increased or the challenge should be decreased until the skills improve. Are there opportunities to increase the challenge when youth respond with apathy or boredom? The outcomes of misaligned skills and challenges can present themselves as behavioral issues. Properly aligning the two concepts can be another tool to help improve youth outcomes.

Equip · Inspire · Impact

- **Encourage youth engagement and success by matching skill and challenge levels in activities.**
- **Prompt youth to become more engaged by practicing mindfulness and leveraging character strengths.**
- **When witnessing behavioral issues, explore the level of engagement the young person may be experiencing.**

Habits

*"Great things are done by a series of
small things brought together."*

— *Vincent Van Gogh*

Habits are important mental shortcuts that enable youth to navigate their daily lives without having to expend unnecessary thought and energy on mundane choices. They are often subconscious and can be almost involuntary. Habits are developed by repeating behaviors, and like many things, they can both serve and undermine young people. When it comes to evaluating habits, Discover You™ identified the three A's: (be) **Aware**, **Adjust**, and **Act**.

> **Aware:** Recognize and assess existing habits. Since many habit-based behaviors stem from the subconscious level, identifying and categorizing them as distinct behaviors can be challenging. It is crucial to differentiate between habits and who a young person is. Through this perspective, youth may be more receptive to changing their habits. A great example of this is that a young person may choose to smoke, but labeling them as a smoker creates a risk of that behavior becoming part of their identity.

Some habits will be more obvious than others. The misuse of substances may be more easily identified than the habit of inactivity. An exercise for youth is to spend a week capturing everything that feels like a habit, whether large or small. They should consider habits and regular behaviors like going directly to their locker when arriving at school, checking their phone as soon as they wake up or as soon as the bell rings, grabbing lunch from the vending machine, calling Grandma on Sundays, vaping with friends while on break, doing homework before dinner, spending four hours every evening on a screen, etc.

Each habit offers different outcomes, some benign, some positive, and others negative. This book discusses various tools that can help evaluate goals to determine which behaviors to keep, remove, or modify, including the Learning Loop from Chapter 3, Social Awareness from Chapter 4, SMART Plus goals from Chapter 5, and the Stages of Change from Chapter 8.

> **Adjust:** Encourage youth to eliminate or replace habits that take them away from their desired state. When it comes to change, social scientist B.J. Fogg said, "I change best by feeling good, not feeling bad." The days have passed when the preferred route to modifying behavior comes from torturing ourselves into changing habits by setting outrageous goals and putting ourselves on punishing regimens. We know from experience that this generally doesn't work for us, and it won't work any better for young people.

How deeply ingrained are our personal beliefs that change is hard, implementing new habits is excruciating, and achieving goals is exhausting? If we believe that change is hard, we will likely convey that belief to our youth. The messages we send are often a result of our personal experiences and beliefs. Too often, our personal habits and thought patterns influence what we model and attempt to teach.

Change, done well, does not have to be difficult or painful. Of course, there will be times when it isn't easy. Habits that do not serve youth and have driven many of their choices can be interrupted and put aside. They can be replaced with behaviors that move youth toward their desired goals. Those are the skills we need to model and present to young people. We explore this later in this section.

Act: Encourage youth to build positive, small habits that move them toward their goals. In his *New York Times* bestselling book, *Tiny Habits*, Fogg suggests that we start by developing Tiny Habits™, using a three-pronged approach that can lead to big change. An example we will explore for clarity is after I brush my teeth every morning and night, I will mentally practice a section of the song I'm learning, and I will celebrate by high-fiving myself in the mirror.

- After I...
- I will...
- And to celebrate...

This is a simple process of choosing an existing routine to anchor a new Tiny Habit to, scaling back a new habit to bite-sized portions, and then providing ourselves with a positive reward. This process is beneficial in building new habits and replacing negative behaviors with positive ones. A Tiny Habit is a behavior you do regularly and can do under most circumstances. Short is good, often less than 30 seconds, and it should require little effort. "After I" allows us to identify anchor behaviors. "I will" is our opportunity to choose a tiny behavior. And "I celebrate" is the necessary component of rewarding ourselves.

Anchor behaviors are the prompts or triggers that influence us regularly, whether we are aware of them or not. According to Fogg, triggers come from a person, context, or action. Person prompts come from the young person and their body, such as hunger or anxiety. Context prompts are reminders such as sticky notes, a meaningful bracelet, or an alarm. Action prompts are things they already do that signal other actions, such as brushing their teeth or turning on the computer. Encourage young people to use triggers to inspire positive change. Don't forget to practice it in your own life first, though.

When young people understand how to control their habits and not let their habits control them, they can move toward their goals and build thriving behaviors.

The key to an anchor that works well in developing Tiny Habits is to use something that already occurs regularly and naturally in a young person's day, such as arriving home from school or eating supper. Encourage young people to identify what they want in the form of a tiny goal or habit. Make it easy, find the right time to perform the behavior, and then celebrate. Starting tiny can lead to success momentum, where these habits, once established, naturally multiply and grow.

In working with young people, we've realized that if they struggle with implementing their new Tiny Habit, they may be able to tweak a few things to achieve greater success. First, is the new behavior something they desire and are motivated for, or is it coming from an external force? As discussed earlier in this chapter, intrinsic motivation and autonomy can drive personal success. Next, consider Fogg's Behavior Model, which suggests that there are five components necessary for making a change: time, money, physical effort, mental effort, and routine. Review each component with the young person and encourage them to identify which area might provide a challenge and plan to overcome it.

"After I..." "I will..." "I celebrate by..." - an ingenious process for developing positive behaviors.

Another approach to habits is presented in James Clear's book, *Atomic Habits*. Clear suggests four laws that young people can leverage to create a good habit:

- **Make it obvious**: Use primers and reminders, such as posting a motivating note or picture in their locker.
- **Make it attractive:** Pair something they need to do with something they want to do, such as pairing their love of music and dance with their goal of getting more exercise.
- **Make it easy:** Reduce external friction and prime the environment by pre-arranging rides to a commitment or ensuring it aligns with their existing schedule.
- **Make it satisfying:** Incorporate reinforcement and rewards, such as the bonus of having fun with their friends.

Clear points out that the inverse also works. Just as there are laws to create a positive habit, there are also four laws to break a negative habit:

- **Make it invisible:** Reduce exposure to it by not leaving school grounds at lunch with their friends who are vaping.
- **Make it unattractive:** Reframe their mindset by focusing on the cons of vaping and how it interferes with goals.
- **Make it difficult:** Place barriers in their own path, such as not having extra cash to purchase the products.
- **Make it unsatisfying:** Get involved in activities where it is difficult to vape.

Habits are important components of our lives, both consciously and subconsciously. When young people understand how to control their habits and not let their habits control them, they can move toward their goals and build thriving behaviors. As a young person gains immediate wins, they gain confidence, which in turn creates a compounding effect.

Equip · Inspire · Impact

- **Encourage young people to evaluate their habits by becoming aware, adjusting those that don't serve them, and acting to build habits that move them closer to their goals.**
- **Promote Tiny Habits using the formula "After I…" "I will…" "Then I will celebrate by…"**
- **Advocate for making new positive habits obvious, attractive, easy, and satisfying.**

Choices

"If you choose not to decide, you still have made a choice."
— *Neil Peart*

Having choices is a young person's ability to select their preference. It is unclear how many choices an average person makes per day. An internet search suggests that there are approximately 35,000 choices made per day; that equates to approximately one choice every two seconds. Choices can range from insignificant to substantial and can be conscious or subconscious. Relatively insignificant choices can occur when a young person is tying a shoe, putting the right lace over the left, then the left over the right, etc. Substantial choices are those that have greater effects, such as whether to drive sober or what to do after high school. Many initially conscious choices become habits, such as when learning to drive, using your blinker moves from a conscious to a subconscious act.

Of those 35,000 daily choices, it is estimated that 122 are significant, although this number is not substantiated either. Those are choices that require greater consideration, presenting themselves at the rate of 7.6 per hour or one every eight minutes. One thing is certain: with so much decision-making, decision fatigue is a real issue for us all. Developing strong personal skills such as confidence, self-efficacy, and a growth mindset can help youth make all these decisions a bit more manageable.

We will explore the different dynamics of choice and how we can help youth make choices that best serve them, using the **Yes or No Option**, the **Paradox of Choice**, and the concepts of **Maximizers and Satisficers**.

The **Yes or No Option** is often used to create the illusion that there are only two options: good or bad, with us or against us, all or nothing. When presented with only two options, the mind tends to instantly pick the best of those two without considering alternatives. When young people realize life rarely gives only two options, they can always look for alternatives, whether they are presented to them or not. Perhaps it is a different option altogether, or a combination of two or more things that will create the best option for them. Here are some examples:

- **Love it or hate it:** Youth may select something with a few small changes or not care either way. They can respect that their school offers extracurricular activities while not having strong feelings in either direction.
- **In or out:** Is there a way for a youth to participate without being fully committed? Is there a middle ground? Can they go back and forth as needed? Perhaps they can be involved when it aligns with their schedule.
- **Support us or hate us:** Not supporting us is not the same as hating us. Is there something else more important to a young person that doesn't align with supporting this? Why can't they both not care about it and not hate it? Just because they aren't vegetarians doesn't mean they don't care about animals. They can advocate for helping endangered species, yet do not want to break the law to show support.

- **Immediate choice:** What happens if they don't choose at all? Can they change their vote later? Can they date and not commit? Do they have to decide this minute?

When given only two options, the hope is that youth will choose the obvious "better" choice without considering the details.

Paradox of Choice, a term coined by psychologist Barry Schwartz, is another issue. The Paradox of Choice suggests that the vast number of choices available makes it more difficult to make a decision and becomes a deterrent to being happy with what we choose. Exploring this with young people can help them understand all the choices and opportunities they are currently facing and why they may be feeling frustrated and anxious. Consider ordering ice cream as an analogy. Would you prefer chocolate or vanilla? That is a clear choice for many. If you were able to choose from 12 different varieties of ice cream, would that make it more difficult to choose? Does it take longer? Once we make a choice, our selection is good until we see what someone else ordered, which may cause us to question our decision. And this is just ice cream.

Consider autonomy as it relates to the paradox of choice. Autonomy is our freedom to make uncoerced choices, which is a critical component of young people's overall wellbeing. Many youth have more available choices than any other group of people has ever had before, and thus, presumably, they have more freedom and autonomy. That seems like a beneficial position to be in, yet we see that all these choices can become paralyzing. The more choices available, the more difficult it can become for young people to make a choice and be content with it. Being fearful of making wrong decisions and the inability to choose can have effects that range from mild to debilitating.

Consider the life-defining choices facing our young adults: which trade school, college, or university to attend, which career path to pursue, which state to live in, whether to choose a partner, whether to purchase a vehicle or use public transportation, and whether to prioritize work or school. All these significant decisions make it imperative to assure young people that it is normal to feel overwhelmed and that they are not alone in feeling this way. It may also be comforting for them to know that in many situations, they can choose again. If they start with one major, they can change their major or future career later. However, making informed choices initially can save time, grief, and money. Remember, although our youth need autonomy, they still often require our support in navigating all the available options and in helping them make the best life choices.

> Life is a series of making choices and experiencing the outcomes of those choices.

Maximizers and Satisficers are two types of decision-makers identified by Schwartz. Understanding this concept may help our young people be more satisfied once they have made a choice.

Maximizers research as many options as possible. They sacrifice time and effort to learning as much as possible about the offer. They consider all the variables, advantages, and weaknesses. When they make a decision, they compare it to the choices of others. The question is always, "Is there anything better out there?" The downside of maximizers is that they often agonize over their choices after they have been made. An upside for maximizers is that they tend to make thoroughly informed decisions.

Satisficers judge their satisfaction by meeting the standards they have set for themselves. They make a decision or take action once their criteria are met. That doesn't mean they settle for mediocrity. Their criteria may be quite high, but they are satisfied as soon as they find what meets their expectations. They aren't prone to revisiting options after they have made a choice. A potential downside for satisficers is that they may not fully explore all of their options and make less-than-ideal choices, but that, too, might be perfectly acceptable.

One way to help young people navigate choices is to have them consider the impact of their decision on their lives, whether it's selecting lunch, planning a vacation, or choosing a college major. Suggest they consider:

- How many and what acceptable options do I wish to investigate?
  - Lunch: tacos, burgers, or pizza
  - Summer vacation: Utah, Florida, or Cancun
  - College major: anything in the medical field
- What is the deadline for the decision?
  - Lunch by 11:00
  - Summer vacation by the weekend
  - College major by fall
- What information is required, and where will I source it from?
  - Lunch something local
  - Vacation by asking my friends and family
  - College majors doing online research.

Once their decision is made, students may be in a position to celebrate the benefits and refrain from further comparison, at least as far as lunch goes. The more complex the decision and the more time involved, the more young people may need to revisit it and adjust as able and necessary.

Suggest youth conduct a Learning Loop from Chapter 3 on their choice. What went well? What did they struggle with or face challenges with? What will they do differently next time? There is no right or wrong way to make decisions. The greater the impact of the choice, the more consideration it requires. An important reminder for our youth is that being a maximizer or satisficer isn't fixed; there are appropriate times and applications for both. Understanding the concept helps young people make better choices and live with them. Encourage young people to trust their instincts, be intentional, and cultivate confidence.

Life is a series of making choices and experiencing the outcomes of those choices. Young people can leverage tools to make good decisions. However, it can be helpful to remind them that they can only make the best choice based on the information that is available to them at the time. Support them with wise guidance and counsel as appropriate. The number of decisions young people need to make, both significant and relatively insignificant, can be overwhelming for them.

Equip · Inspire · Impact

- **Encourage young people to explore additional options beyond those presented to them.**
- **Normalize how overwhelming it can feel to have a wide array of choices and help set realistic goals surrounding the number of choices to consider.**
- **Remind young people to focus on what is in their control when making choices.**

Chapter 9

Intention

*"Now tell me, what is it you plan to do with
your one wild and precious life?"*

— *Mary Oliver*

To act with intention is to behave deliberately and purposefully, which is this book's premise. We view intention as acting with a purpose in mind. Intention can be viewed in the context of investing today for rewards tomorrow. It can manifest itself as delaying gratification by saying no to ice cream for better future health, studying for a test instead of attending a party, or planting a tree for which one won't see the benefits for years. Intention is about planning and making conscious choices that will lead us to where we want to be in the future; it is similar to having a strategic plan.

Imagine being on a cruise ship in the middle of the ocean. Looking around the glamorous dining room, you notice guests enjoying dinner with the captain and the entire crew. You approach the captain and inquire who is steering the ship, to which he replies, "No one. We are on an adventure and will see where we end up."

Without direction or intention, the cruise ship will likely face many unintended consequences, such as navigating into severe storms, depleting food and water supplies, and running aground somewhere long before reaching any port. Yet, we often do with our lives what we would never dream of doing on a vacation cruise.

An example of intention is when my children were young, we held a generalized assumption that they would attend post-secondary education. We didn't discuss "if" they would attend, but "when" and "where" they would attend. It was never forced, but a presumption that once you leave high school, additional career education is something you do.

> Living with intention can reduce some of the noise that develops around young people.

Living with intention can reduce some of the noise that develops around young people. The noise is the distractions and short-term gratification opportunities that abound. It might include risky behaviors such as substance misuse, driving recklessly, or questionable relationships. Knowing the intentional goal can provide enough support to sift out some of the risk-taking opportunities that may present themselves. Without intention or direction, many things can sound intriguing in the moment, with few of them leading young people to where they hope to be.

In the last chapter, we discussed choices. When a youth's choices are intentional, they're thought through and are more likely to lead to fewer negative outcomes. That's the goal. Just like resiliency isn't gained through happenstance, but is in deciding or intentionally making it through to the other side of whatever is hurting or holding them back. If youth aren't steering their boat, they allow the tides and the wind to dictate. How do we intentionally help young people build intentional lives? When young people slow down, reflect, and decide, they practice intention and exert more control over their life's direction.

Equip · Inspire · Impact

- **Engage in a conversation with a young person, focusing on their life goals and intentions.**
- **Ask a young person in what areas they are intentionally delaying gratification today to build for tomorrow.**
- **Encourage young people to consider their future intentions when faced with noise and distractions.**

Responsible Decision-Making

*"Life is a chess match. Every decision that
you make has a consequence to it."*
— P.K. Subban

According to the Collaborative for Academic, Social, and Emotional Learning, referenced in the Evidence-Based Frameworks section, responsible decision-making is the ability to make caring and constructive choices about personal behavior and social interactions across diverse situations. This includes making choices about personal behavior and social interactions based on ethical standards, safety concerns, and social norms. Responsible decisions entail the realistic evaluation of the consequences of various actions and consideration of the wellbeing of oneself and others. We generally recognize the importance of making good and thoughtful decisions. As adults who impact youth, encouraging responsible decision-making is a top priority.

Due to various factors, including brain development, young people may tend to prioritize immediate gratification over long-term benefits. Immediate gratification is when one chooses a gain in the immediate or short term at the expense of a future or long-term gain. It is the desire to experience some sort of pleasure or gain without delay. The pace at which our world moves promotes the idea of immediate and instant gratification. We microwave dinners, skim communications, and rush from one

> Young people need to be cognizant of their own needs and those of the people around them, ultimately prioritizing decisions that lead to prosocial outcomes.

activity to the next. Those types of decisions do not always pair well with responsible decision-making. Unfortunately, many early life decisions can impact young people long into their future.

Numerous skills and behaviors support responsible decision-making and demonstrate a progression toward making good decisions. Some things for young people to consider might be:

- Are they demonstrating curiosity and open-mindedness?
- Are they identifying solutions for personal and social problems?
- Are they analyzing information and seeking facts?
- Can they anticipate and evaluate the consequences of their actions?
- Are they recognizing how critical thinking skills are helpful in all aspects of their lives?
- Are they considering and evaluating personal, interpersonal, familial, communal, and institutional impacts?

Deandra will demonstrate steps that can be taken to help make responsible decisions.

Clearly define the pending decision. Deandra is in her second year of college and struggling financially. She is trying to decide whether to finish college or pursue a full-time career.

Consider the impact of this decision. The greater the impact, the more crucial the process. Deandra recognizes that this decision will affect her finances, time, family, career, present, and future.

Gather information. The greater the decision, the more time should be spent on this step. Deandra visits her college advisor to learn about financial aid. She also talks to her aunt, who completed college and has a good job, and considers her current budget and opportunities for career advancement.

Explore alternatives. Deandra looks at trade schools, colleges, and universities. She considers her career options and potential earnings should she not complete post-secondary education. She is reminded that one advantage of finishing school is the increased likelihood of financial security. One disadvantage is the challenges she will face supporting herself in the present.

Weigh the evidence. Objectively and fairly evaluate the information to help minimize preconceived ideas about possible outcomes. Deandra asks herself if she has fully considered the consequences of quitting college and wonders if her present state of exhaustion makes that idea more appealing. She decides to conduct a more thorough assessment before making her decision.

Choose. Considering all things, make the best choice. Deandra chooses to complete college.

Take intentional action. Deandra registers for next semester's classes and makes a list of additional actions she needs to take.

Review the decision. Deandra asks herself:

- Did it work out as hoped?
- What were the consequences?
- Does any component need to be reconsidered?
- Was any key information not considered initially?
- How did (or did not) the actions or decisions solve or address the problem?
- What did you do to evaluate the situation?
- When you reflect on the situation, what do you determine?

Deandra evaluates the outcomes at the end of the semester, determines she made the correct choice, makes a few adjustments, and continues to work toward her degree.

Responsible decision-making is a combination of awareness and intention. Young people need to be cognizant of their own needs and those of the people around them, ultimately prioritizing decisions that lead to prosocial outcomes. As adults who impact youth, we play a key role in supporting their decision-making, whether it is through a well-worded and timely question or walking a young person through the potential outcomes of a decision.

Equip · Inspire · Impact

- Support young people in responsible decision-making by accurately articulating what decision needs to be made and the desired outcomes.
- Engage in a conversation that explores the impacts of a decision both on the young person and those around them.
- Conduct a Learning Loop with young people to facilitate easy evaluation of a decision.

ABC DE FG Model

"The problem is not the problem.
The problem is your attitude about the problem."
— *Jack Sparrow, Pirates of the Caribbean*

The narrative we tell ourselves and the beliefs we hold influence how situations unfold. When young people accept personal responsibility for their role in a situation, they increase their likelihood of seeing it accurately and experiencing beneficial outcomes.

The **ABC DE FG** Model provides a process for a young person to consider how their beliefs about a situation directly affect the outcome of that situation, allowing space to challenge those beliefs.

A: The Activating event is something that happened.

B: The Belief is our young person's opinion about the situation, the story they tell themselves.

C: The Consequence is the result following the emotion or behavior exhibited that is directly related to their belief.

DE: Dispute with Evidence is to intentionally dispute or challenge the beliefs and look for evidence to support or negate the belief.

FG: Fixed versus Growth mindset is about recognizing whether a fixed or growth mindset is present and reminding youth to engage the growth mindset approach.

We have Holly, a 13-year-old aspiring actress, who wasn't chosen for a role in the school play to demonstrate this model. That is the Activating event. For this example, we consider three different beliefs Holly could hold regarding the event.

Belief One: "The director doesn't like me, so they picked someone else." The consequence of that belief is that since the director doesn't like her, Holly begins speaking badly about the theatrical program. She tries out for another play in the future, but she doesn't get chosen. Not getting chosen a second time reinforces Holly's beliefs about the director.

> Attitudes and beliefs about situations are directly related to the outcome of the situation.

Did Holly dispute this with evidence? Did she speak with the director or consider other possible causes? She did not. If she had, she may have found evidence contradicting her belief. Holly's approach was to adopt a fixed mindset, assuming the director was bad, thus she wasn't chosen.

Belief Two: Holly believes her friend Josh sabotaged her and that she deserved the role, but he spread rumors about her, so she didn't get it. The consequence of that belief is that since Holly believes Josh sabotaged her, she begins saying mean things about him and quits hanging out with him. Josh is confused and doesn't understand why his friend turned on him, so he begins to hang out with other people and speaks negatively about Holly. Due to Josh's negative comments and actions, Holly is convinced she is right, and their friendship is over.

Did Holly dispute this with evidence? Did she hear Josh saying things herself or talk to him directly? Did she explore other possible causes for not being chosen? If she had, she would have found evidence contradicting her belief. Again, Holly had a fixed mindset response as she determined Josh behaved badly and didn't explore opportunities to challenge that.

Belief Three: Brittney, who got the part, was better qualified than she was. That can be hard for anyone to admit, but let's join Holly as she discovers the consequences of that belief. Holly accepts that Brittney is clearly a good choice for the part and chooses to stay engaged with the theater. She builds relationships with the other performers and the director, picks up tips, and becomes recognized as a helpful and important part of the theatrical team.

Did Holly dispute this with evidence? Yes, once she put her emotions aside and looked at the situation objectively, she realized that Brittney was a good choice. Belief Three embraced a growth mindset as Holly explored ways to grow and become more engaged. She took this failure as an opportunity to fail well and learn. As a result, when it came time to audition for the next play, Holly got the part.

To clarify, Holly could have chosen Belief Three, accepted Brittney as the better choice, and leveraged a growth mindset, but it would not have led to her desired outcome. Encouraging our youth to challenge their beliefs does not guarantee positive outcomes, but ensures they are making informed decisions. It also reminds them that just because they believe something to be true does not make it so.

The **ABC DE FG** model encourages youth to challenge their beliefs and, more importantly, recognize that what they believe directly affects their behavior. How they behave directly affects the outcomes of a situation. Often, young people feel that the outcomes of situations are a direct result of the situation itself. That they are victims or powerless when things happen. This thought process encourages blame and helplessness, rarely benefiting the individual in the end. We just demonstrated that a young person has a tremendous amount of influence on how situations in their lives unfold.

Attitudes and beliefs about situations are directly related to the outcome of the situation. Young people must understand the influence they have on their lives and the consequences of their beliefs and actions. It is essential that we help them challenge the narratives they tell themselves and recognize their intentionality in shaping their lives.

Equip · Inspire · Impact

- **Share the ABC DE FG Model to demonstrate the impact a young person's belief has on the outcome of a situation.**
- **Encourage personal responsibility and ownership in challenging situations.**
- **When a young person faces a challenging situation, work through the model together, changing their beliefs to demonstrate how different the outcomes can be.**

Self-Management

"The willingness to accept responsibility for one's own life is the source from which self-respect springs."
— *Joan Didion*

According to the Collaborative for Academic, Social, and Emotional Learning, referenced in the Evidence-Based Frameworks section, self-management is the ability to manage one's emotions, thoughts, and behaviors effectively in different situations and to achieve goals and aspirations. It includes abilities such as:

- Managing emotions by leveraging them to inform behavior, not direct it.
- Identifying and using stress-management strategies by managing stress to the degree it does not cause undue interference in one's life.
- Exhibiting self-discipline and self-motivation by controlling responses to situations and being intrinsically motivated.
- Setting personal and collective goals by working for the betterment of self and community.

- Using planning and organizational skills to achieve goals by leveraging knowledge and abilities.
- Showing courage to take the initiative by a willingness to lead and engage in healthy risk-taking.
- Demonstrating personal and collective agency by understanding how much is in one's control.
- Managing time and resources by using what is available to achieve the best outcomes.

When youth are able to self-manage, we see increased success throughout their lives, including in academics, extracurricular activities, and relationships. These skills also benefit youth by increasing their confidence and making them more thoughtful and present in their interactions.

As we consider young people's futures, these are critical skills employers are seeking to adapt to an ever-changing world with shifting demands. Employers are seeking emotionally mature employees who can behave professionally and make positive contributions to a team. We can help young people develop self-management skills by:

- Encouraging emotional management with an emphasis on benefiting, not harming, themselves and others.
- Helping them find ways to stay in control, particularly when emotions run high, be they stressful or celebratory.
- Helping them have high personal standards that move them toward being the best version of themselves and meeting their goals.
- Encouraging adaptability in thinking and acting.
- Assisting them in developing a growth mindset.
- Promoting the understanding and use of their personal character strengths.

Skill development often begins with awareness and conversation. At The ROCK, one tactic we use to explore these skills with young people is watching a movie together. We set the stage by choosing two characters on which the youth are encouraged to focus. One of the characters exhibits high levels of self-management, and the other does not. Then we debrief the movie with talking points such as:

- What are examples of the character's self-management or lack thereof?
- How did the character's degree of self-management affect those around them?
- How did the character's degree of self-management affect the character personally?
- What are three things the character lacking self-management could do to improve?
- How does it feel to watch someone not in control of themselves?

Self-management is all about choices, and it begins with self- or emotional awareness, which we explored in Chapter 5. Young people need to understand that, although they cannot control everything in life, there are many things they can control—themselves and their reactions, first and foremost. They also need to realize that their behaviors are their responsibility, regardless of the circumstances leading up to them. This sense of personal influence can help our young people maintain control over their own lives.

Accepting personal responsibility is a crucial aspect of self-management. We can help youth develop self-management through accountability. Consider self-management in relation to the distinction between reasons and excuses. For example, a young person is regularly late for sports practice. Workarounds may be made when there are legitimate reasons, such as those related to transportation. Although there are likely still consequences, the approach and outcome stem from a place of responsibility.

However, if the tardiness is related to hanging out with friends and not coming directly to practice, any reason for being late becomes an excuse. The adults in their lives might better serve the young person by holding them accountable and expecting them to meet these standards. Excuses do not remove personal responsibility. Having an excuse for something that did or did not happen doesn't change the fact that something did not go as intended.

Jason demonstrates excuses nicely. Jason drives to school and consistently arrives late. He enters his first-hour class with an excuse he has prepared in advance.

When youth are able to self-manage, we see increased success throughout their lives, including in academics, extracurricular activities, and relationships.

The first few times, Mr. Russell attempted to help Jason resolve the situation and gave him a pass. As it continued, Jason began receiving marks against his attendance. When Jason confronted Mr. Russell, he was told the reason for his tardiness didn't matter; he was still expected to attend class on time like everyone else.

Jason's flippant response that he couldn't plan for every flat tire (though there likely never was one) was rebuked with, "This is your responsibility, and you need to find a way to succeed. Or I am happy to provide the opportunity for you to see if you are timelier during summer school." Jason found a way to be on time for Mr. Russell's class.

The teacher's advice was direct and straightforward. Excuses may buy young people a few passes, but ultimately, it comes down to personal responsibility and the results that follow. We must be cautious not to accept excuses too often. Young people are more than capable of reaching reasonably high expectations when provided with the opportunity. We can support youth in building realistic success plans using SMART Plus goals, which include backup plans, as discussed in Chapter 5. Self-management is the path to achieving one's goals and aspirations. When young people demonstrate responsibility, new doors open for them.

Equip · Inspire · Impact

- **Create a culture of accountability where young people address problems using a solutions approach and assume personal responsibility.**
- **Watch a movie with a young person and evaluate the character's level of self-management. Encourage the young person to identify actions the character could take to increase self-management.**
- **Set reasonably high standards for young people and guide them to meet them.**

Self

"You are what you believe yourself to be."
— *Paulo Coelho*

A strong sense of self helps young people maintain their mental, physical, and emotional wellbeing. Combined with an inward healthy love and respect, our youth can become their own best selves. We will explore the following list of self-concepts, which is extensive but not conclusive:

- **Self-centeredness**
- **Self-esteem**
- **Self-worth**
- **Self-care**
- **Self-compassion**
- **Self-acceptance**
- **Self-respect**

Self-centeredness: Each person is appropriately at the center of their world and should maintain a healthy balance in relation to others. When self-centeredness becomes excessive, it gives rise to an overinflated sense of self, relative to the world and the people around them. It occurs when one's concern is inner-focused, with

The goal of building assets in youth is to help young people develop a healthy sense of self so they see themselves as balanced and important parts of the universe and contribute to the betterment of the world while living healthy and productive lives.

the priority being getting one's own needs met to an extreme level, expecting one's interests to be everyone's priority.

Self-esteem: When young people have self-esteem, they like or care about themselves; they're confident and satisfied with themselves. Self-esteem is the good feeling component of self-worth. The work doesn't end there, though. One of the limits of self-esteem is that youth can like themselves until something goes wrong, and then they don't. Another is that it can be predicated on others' opinions of them, which can be fleeting and even dangerous. It is important for young people to have more than self-esteem. They also need, among other traits, a sense of self-worth.

Self-worth: Self-worth is when youth believe they have value. When they bring something important to the table and believe they have something necessary for someone else, it increases their sense of value as human beings. Each individual determines their own personal self-worth, which is a crucial point. True strengths are only strengths because they are personally perceived as such. Relying on someone else to validate them removes an individual's personal power and self-worth. When young people have self-worth, the opinions of others don't affect them nearly as much. Self-worth makes them stronger, so they are less likely to tolerate negative treatment or, at the very least, be as adversely affected by it.

Self-worth empowers young people to better withstand peer pressure, as they are less likely to relinquish their power to others.

Self-worth is present when one no longer requires validation from others or feels the need to please them. Consequently, they control how they feel about themselves. Their contributions don't have to be monumental; they can be as simple as recognizing their impact at home, such as knowing that the chores they complete and the dinners they prepare contribute to the family's success.

Self-compassion: When youth practice self-compassion, they treat themselves with kindness and respect. It is an act of befriending themselves. Self-compassion involves giving oneself a break, affirming oneself, and accepting mistakes and imperfections. Practicing self-compassion involves using positive self-talk and treating oneself with kindness and understanding, much like one would a good friend. With self-compassion, our youth will recognize that they are better at some things than others and accept that fact. When they make a mistake, they don't dwell on it negatively, but instead commit to doing better.

Self-care: Self-care is a combination of intentional behaviors, actions, and attitudes that prioritize personal physical, mental, social, spiritual, and emotional wellbeing. This is where self-compassion moves into action. When youth practice self-care, they prioritize physically healthy behaviors, such as consuming quality food, staying hydrated, and getting enough rest. They avoid high-risk behaviors such as drug and alcohol misuse, risky sex, or driving while intoxicated or distracted. Young people who practice self-care will also prioritize their emotional, mental, and spiritual wellbeing by avoiding toxic people and relationships, seeking help when needed, and considering their needs equal to those of others. They know how to say no to strangers or close friends when appropriate.

Self-acceptance: It is essential for youth to develop self-acceptance, which can be easier for some than for others. They can and should recognize the aspects of themselves that serve them well and those areas they need to improve. Youth can acknowledge and accept their fears, flaws, and negative behaviors for what they are. They don't need to take pride in them, but should grant themselves the grace to address them. When youth accept themselves for who they are, they can better forgive themselves without harsh judgment. Self-acceptance fosters a sense of peace and confidence.

Self-respect: Of all the people and things to respect in this world, young people should begin with themselves. They should first and foremost honor themselves, holding themselves in high regard. They need to extend themselves kindness, tolerance, generosity, compassion, and love. Self-respect sounds like: "I care about myself enough to know this relationship isn't good for me." "I have worked hard and will enjoy going out tonight." "I deserve to be treated well and am worthy of love."

You can teach and model positive self-talk to help youth develop a strong sense of self-respect. When you notice them speaking negatively about themselves, suggest reframing the statement. For example, turn "I am so dumb" into "I am learning new things." Chapter 1 covered reframing in more depth.

If you witness youth mistreating themselves via lack of sleep, nutrition, or substance misuse, have a conversation with them. An excellent way to frame it is: "How would you feel if someone you cared about behaved that way?" "Would it be beneficial to their future?" "What would you suggest they do in place of those behaviors?"

The goal of building assets in youth is to help young people develop a healthy sense of self so they see themselves as balanced and important parts of the universe and contribute to the betterment of the world while living healthy and productive lives. There is no shortcut to doing the work and living life together. All the trophies, trinkets, and trite comments won't replace the important cores. And those tokens won't help young people discover true and lasting value within themselves.

A strong sense of self can contribute to increased confidence, resilience, and courage. Understanding who one is and being comfortable with one's worth can help one fail well and develop a growth mindset. Knowing oneself can help our youth manage and understand their emotions and behaviors. A young person may be better prepared for healthy and challenging relationships when they possess a strong sense of self. As a trusted adult, foster in youth their ability to have a healthy balance between themselves and those around them.

Equip · Inspire · Impact

- **Encourage young people to develop a positive sense of self.**
- **Hold young people accountable for self-care.**
- **Assist young people in reframing negative self-talk to language that is supportive.**

Conclusion

*"You're never ready for what you
have to do. You just do it.
That makes you ready."*

— *Flora Rheta Schreiber*

More than 20 years ago, I received an invitation that would change everything I thought about youth and how to serve them. At the time, I wasn't working with youth. In fact, I was a single mom, struggling to make ends meet. But I wanted the best for my children. At the insistence of my son, Thomas, my daughter, Nichole, and my husband, Kevin, I answered the call to become the president of The ROCK. Along the way, I challenged myself to develop the skills and assets that would help me succeed. I became a disrupter who, paired with a remarkable team, felt empowered to make the changes our youth needed. Together, we developed life-changing programs that shifted the industry and made a lasting impact.

From my experience, I can tell you that anyone with a desire and willingness can make a difference. It doesn't matter where you come from or how unlikely a candidate you seem to be for influencing youth. Your unique gifts, talents, and skills make you the perfect person. Coupled with the strategies and inspiration throughout the pages of this book, I truly believe you will be the asset builder you have always wanted to be. And our youth need you.

You may not feel prepared to start the work; please don't let that deter you, as you will never be 100% ready. During my tenure at The ROCK and Discover You™, I have learned to make the best possible decisions based on the available information and move forward. Two things may occur if you wait until you believe you are 100% prepared. First, you will miss the opportunity to help likely hundreds of young people and save at least a few lives, some of whom may be literally saved. Second, if you view your plans at 100%, you may think you have it figured out and perhaps miss situations where you need to flex. You are working with young people and systems that will always require adapting plans and projects. There will always be opportunities to refine your message and program. That is the process of doing. Please do not let the idea of perfection or being fully prepared stand in your way. Do something today: take action on a small scale with the one youth in your immediate path, or do it on a grand scale for thousands.

Here are some thoughts to consider as you move forward:

- **Challenge the systems**: Many of you may not be in high-functioning systems, but have still chosen to do the work. Despite the frustrations that can come with this, continue seeking solutions. I hope this book will help you create the change you seek.
- **Develop assets in youth and yourself:** Youth must have the tools we discussed throughout this book to thrive when they can and struggle well when needed. We explored the assets youth need to succeed: hope, strength, resilience, courage, confidence, connection, purpose, motivation, and intention. Transferring these skills to youth is most effective when you first develop these assets in yourself.

- **Celebrate the wins:** Throughout my career, I have witnessed individuals and organizations make changes and incorporate the strategies in this book. Within those organizations, I have been inspired by countless individuals who have demonstrated courage and care as they provide support to young people. These individuals have been able to create real change despite the noise. As a result, they have changed the world for youth. I believe you are likely one of those people and encourage you to celebrate your wins, big and small, along your journey.
- **Empower youth:** Young people need to find peace and worth inside themselves. As adults who have the privilege of ushering in the next generations, our role is to guide, support, and direct. This requires us to resist doing the work for them. Otherwise, we will deny young people the experiences that enable them to develop the grit, resilience, and strength necessary for them to thrive in life.

Thank you for joining me on this journey. Throughout these pages, we have explored a wide range of attitudes, beliefs, skills, and behaviors that, individually and collectively, strengthen our youth. This book serves as a resource that allows any section to be re-examined as necessary. The concepts here are as important and timeless as your commitment to working with young people. During our time together, I hope you have gained an abundance of knowledge, ideas, and inspiration to be a change agent in the lives of young people. The most powerful thing you can do is begin.

- **Every kid, everywhere:** That's when our work is finished— when every kid, everywhere, has the resources, support, knowledge, and skills to thrive when they can and struggle well when they need to. Until then, you and I have a lot of work to do.

Let's Keep In Touch...

This is just the beginning of the journey, and we would love to keep in touch with you. Please share your tales of success and trial, wins and fails, which are guaranteed to inspire us all. Visit us at **discoveryou.org** or email our team at **impact@discoveryou.org** and use the subject line "*Discover You*th work with us."

Evidence-Based Frameworks

The first iteration of Discover You™ was created based on what I wanted for my own children, things I hoped I had done, things I wished I had done, and things I knew I had missed entirely. It wasn't researched in books, it didn't contain flow charts, and the opinions of others were not solicited. It was thoroughly researched by the director of a youth program, who lived among thousands of teens and drew on the instincts of a mother.

Although the programs were supported by science and research shortly following their inception, gut feelings and rapid implementation in the field came first. It has been more than a 20-year journey, with our programs continually being field-tested by thousands of youth and hundreds of adults. I must say, I am proud of our groundbreaking model and the strong reputation it has garnered. But even more so, I am proud of the youth and adults who have benefited from our earnest efforts.

Our Discover You™ Program Development Model yields the desired outcomes that include:

- **Resilient youth with thriving levels of Developmental Assets and lower levels of risk-taking behavior.** This is accomplished by helping youth demonstrate social and emotional learning competencies and leveraging the tools

RESILIENT YOUTH
·····························
INCREASED DEVELOPMENTAL ASSETS

IMPACTFUL ADULTS
·····························
DEVELOPMENTAL RELATIONSHIPS

DISCOVER YOU™
·····························
PROGRAMS AND TRAININGS

TOOLS OF
APPLIED POSITIVE
PSYCHOLOGY

COMPETENCIES OF
SOCIAL EMOTIONAL
LEARNING

of applied positive psychology. Discover You™ has created a series of age-appropriate workshops to achieve this.

- **Impactful adults who foster the development of the youth through Developmental Relationships and intentional skill-building.** To develop impactful adults competent in creating Developmental Relationships, Discover You™ trains them through several pathways, including effectively delivering Discover You™ workshops to youth. Adults gain from the same evidence-based frameworks that support the development of youth. We explore the frameworks later in this section.

The approach shared in *Discover You*th the book, and Discover You™ the program, is considered a Tier 1 mental health intervention. According to the National Center for School Mental Health, Tier 1 services and support are mental health-related activities designed to meet the needs of all students regardless of their level of risk for mental health problems.

Tier 1 activities promote positive social, emotional, and behavioral skills and wellbeing. These activities also include efforts to support staff wellbeing, improve the school or program climate, and promote positive behavior. These activities can be implemented school-wide, at the grade level, and/or at the classroom level, in out-of-school-time, and can be provided by both organization/ school-employed and community-employed, or school-based professionals.

When we started Discover You™, our goal was not to create a Tier 1 mental health intervention but to provide tools that make young people mentally strong, resilient, and agile. Along the way, we discovered that the National Center for School Mental Health Tier 1 services aligned with our goals. Furthermore, we found that both of our respective objectives are accomplished through similar skills developed in youth.

Discover You™, like other programs, becomes a Tier 2 mental health intervention when used in situations where individuals demand greater support. This could include developing skills to reduce school suspensions or addressing specific challenges, such as those faced by individuals in foster care.

The concepts shared in this book do not reflect new initiatives so much as a unified approach to the whole person. The skills, behaviors, and knowledge in Discover You™ support and enhance the efforts of suicide prevention, mental health and wellbeing, anti-bullying, trauma-informed care, anti-violence, inclusion, equity, the management and prevention of adverse childhood experiences (ACEs), and many more.

The evidence-based frameworks that best align with the Discover You™ Program we developed are:

- **Developmental Assets by Search Institute**
- **Developmental Relationships by Search Institute**
- **Applied Positive Psychology and the science of wellbeing**
- **Social and Emotional Learning**

I am proud of the work these researchers have done and appreciate the value and validity they bring to our efforts. The work at Discover You™ has been strongly influenced by the work of these researchers and others like them.

Developmental Assets

"Young people are not problems to be solved. They are more than the challenges they face. Every single young person contains the seeds of success and thriving." This powerful and insightful comment is from

Search Institute, which has focused on positive youth behaviors since the late 1980s.

Developmental Assets, a research-based framework developed by Search Institute, are the building blocks of healthy development that help young people grow into healthy, caring, and responsible individuals. Research from the Search Institute demonstrates that the more Developmental Assets a young person possesses, the more likely they are to employ thriving prosocial behaviors. Those with fewer assets are more likely to participate in risky behaviors. The Developmental Assets are 40 research-based, positive experiences, skills, values, and qualities grouped into four external and four internal categories.

External Assets:

- **Support:** provided by family and other adults.
- **Empowerment:** where young people feel valued and safe.
- **Boundaries and Expectations:** including clear rules and consequences.
- **Constructive Use of Time:** supportive and prosocial activities.

Internal Assets:

- **Commitment to Learning:** an interest in continued learning.
- **Positive Values:** possession of strong guiding values and principles.
- **Social Competencies:** such as decision-making and interpersonal skills.
- **Positive Identity:** a sense of self and personal control.

In 2009, when we began building our Discover You™ program, The Legacy Center for Community Success, a local nonprofit organization, was currently engaged in a partnership with Search Institute to measure Developmental Assets in middle and high school students throughout the county. The fact that they were measuring assets intrigued me, as it aligned with the strength-based component of the program we were creating. The Developmental Assets would become a core tool, as they provided the language and mechanism we needed to adopt for effective change. In partnership, we measured the impact of our programs on youth with outcomes that revealed statistically relevant increases in all eight categories of Developmental Assets for our participants.

Developmental Relationships

According to Search Institute, *"Everyone is an Asset Builder."* Healthy adult relationships are crucial to positive youth development and contribute to youth experiencing increased social and emotional learning. Those beneficial relationships also play a strong role in youth developing the skills of wellbeing, as discussed in the applied positive psychology section. Lastly, caring and supportive adults promote the development of the aforementioned Developmental Assets.

While programs are an important component of youth development, relationships are key. Programs can provide a framework for conversations and activities, but a program without a caring adult to implement it is far less effective.

Peter L. Benson, former CEO of Search Institute, said, "After decades of forming hypotheses, conducting surveys, crafting and rewriting definitions, analyzing data, and writing journal articles, Search Institute researchers and practitioners have arrived at a surprisingly simple conclusion: Nothing has more impact in the life of a child than positive relationships."

Within Discover You™, we leverage the Developmental

Relationship Framework, created by Search Institute, to guide and measure positive relationships. This includes the five elements that make relationships. They are as follows:

- **Express Care:** demonstrate that the young person matters to you.
- **Challenge Growth:** encourage improvement.
- **Provide Support:** provide appropriate assistance when needed.
- **Share Power:** provide youth with a voice and respect.
- **Expand Possibilities:** make connections and provide opportunities.

One way to be the appropriate relationship-building adult who builds Developmental Assets in youth is to partner with them in their life. Don't simply manage their life. In other words, "do life with them." When my children were young, I worked outside the home. I recall how tired I would be returning home, disheartened by spending my day away from them, as I missed the opportunity to share in many of their milestones. I was also disappointed that I was often too exhausted to be fully engaged in child-centered activities.

To combat the issue, I decided to do the ordinary things together that were already on my to-do list as a mom. We would collectively do chores and home maintenance projects. I initially thought that they might feel this was a punishment, but they beamed at the opportunity to be included and contribute to our home. Our relationships and home flourished. They began taking great pride in our home, and I noticed they also seemed to have a stronger sense of confidence. Another benefit was that this time together allowed us to truly talk to each other, as I wasn't distracted by the tasks that needed to be done around the house. I could give them greater attention, making them feel more cared for and all of us, more connected.

This simple method of collaboration between youth and adults can be implemented in any setting and in any relationship dynamic. The positive lifelong outcomes are endless. Youth will grow up better prepared to care for themselves and will possess the intrinsic motivation to do so compared to their peers who did not have these opportunities in their formative years. That is the throughline of this effort: to help our youth develop into skilled adults who are equipped with the assets they need to thrive.

Applied Positive Psychology

As mentioned previously, positive psychology is the science of human flourishing. Most of us are familiar with traditional psychology, which takes a deficit approach similar to traditional medicine, focusing on fixing what is wrong with us. The concept is that it takes us from sad to not sad, or from sick to not sick. Be assured that this element of traditional medicine and psychology is critical and necessary. However, it is only part of the solution, as proactive measures are also necessary. Concurrently, we can work with positive psychology, which is focused on the strengths that enable humans and organizations to flourish. Positive psychology moves us from a deficit-based mindset that is often imposed upon youth to an asset- or strength-based approach, where the focus is on what they do have. This mindset and methodology greatly support our youth's wellbeing.

Martin Seligman, one of the founders of positive psychology, identified five pillars of wellbeing known as PERMA.

- **Positive Emotions:** the sense of feeling good
- **Engagement:** being invested in our own lives
- **Relationships:** having authentic connections
- **Meaning and Purpose:** a sense of a purposeful existence

- **Accomplishment:** a sense of achieving something noteworthy

This sixth pillar is accepted by many:

- **Health and Vitality:** a sense of strength and energy

Enhancing wellbeing isn't a straightforward journey and varies from person to person. Dr. Michelle McQuaid and Dr. Peggy Kern suggest that thriving involves nurturing each of the PERMAH pillars. The focus and results will differ for each individual, depending on their unique circumstances and choices.

Social and Emotional Learning

Social and Emotional Learning (SEL) focuses on personal growth and development, recognizing that youth require social and emotional skills to thrive and learn. The commonly accepted five core competencies of social and emotional learning are:

- **Self-Awareness:** knowing your strengths and limitations
- **Self-Management:** effectively managing yourself and your emotions
- **Social Awareness:** understanding the perspectives of others
- **Relationship Skills:** interacting appropriately and communicating clearly
- **Responsible Decision-Making:** making constructive choices

As you can see, significant research supports the need to develop these skills in young people and foster developmental relationships. When one combines the four frameworks, it can feel like a "Yes! That is what our youth need!" There are areas of overlap between the frameworks that affirm the constructs independently and collectively. You likely noticed that relationships are a significant component of each construct, which validates the important role you, as educators, family members, and mentors, play in the lives of youth. Your involvement is not only beneficial but also integral to the process.

Resource List

Part I: Hope. Strength. Resilience.

Chapter 1: Hope

Beck, A. T. (1979). *Cognitive therapy of depression*. Guilford Press.

Brinco, E. (2023). *The performance paradox: Turning the power of mindset into action*. Ballantine Books.

Brown, B. (2021). *Atlas of the heart: Mapping meaningful connection and the language of human experience*. Random House.

David, S. (2016). *Emotional agility: Get unstuck, embrace change, and thrive in work and life*. Avery.

Dweck, C. S. (2007). *Mindset: The new psychology of success*. Random House.

Emmons, R. A. (2007). *Thanks! How the new science of gratitude can make you happier*. Houghton Mifflin Harcourt.

Fredrickson, B. L. (2009). *Positivity: Top-notch research reveals the three-to-one ratio that will change your life*. Harmony.

Reivich, K., & Shatté, A. (2002). *The resilience factor: Seven keys to finding your inner strength and overcoming life's hurdles*. Broadway Books.

Seligman, M. E. P. (2018). *The hope circuit: A psychologist's journey from helplessness to optimism.* PublicAffairs.

Snyder, C. R. (1994). *The psychology of hope: You can get there from here.* Free Press.

Van der Kolk, B. (2014). *The body keeps the score: Brain, mind, and body in the healing of trauma.* Viking.

Chapter 2: Strength

Bandura, A. (1997). *Self-efficacy: The exercise of control.* Cambridge University Press.

Linley, A. (2008). *Average to A+: Realising strengths in yourself and others.* CAPP Press.

Niemiec, R. M., & McGrath, R. E. (2019). *The power of character strengths: Appreciate and ignite your positive personality.* VIA Institute on Character.

Peterson, C., & Seligman, M. E. P. (2004). *Character strengths and virtues: A handbook and classification.* Oxford University Press.

Seligman, M. E. P. (2018). *The hope circuit: A psychologist's journey from helplessness to optimism.* PublicAffairs.

Tsang, S. K. M., Hui, E. K. P., & Law, B. C. M. (2012). Self-efficacy as a positive youth development construct: A conceptual review. *The Scientific World Journal.* https://doi.org/10.1100/2012/452327

Chapter 3: Resilience

Duckworth, A. (2016). *Grit: The power of passion and perseverance.* Scribner.

McArdle, M. (2014). *The up side of down: Why failing well is the key to success.* Penguin Books.

Miller, C. A. (2017). *Getting grit: The evidence-based approach to cultivating passion, perseverance, and purpose.* Sounds True.

Saujani, R. (2019). *Brave, not perfect: Fear less, fail more, and live bolder.* Currency.

The Wellbeing Lab. (n.d.). Learning loop. The Wellbeing Lab. https://www.michellemcquaid.com

Part II: Courage. Confidence. Connection

Chapter 4: Courage

Collaborative for Academic, Social, and Emotional Learning (CASEL). (2023, October 24). *Supporting parent and family engagement to enhance students' academic, social, and emotional learning.* https://casel.org/policy-brief-fce-2023Faber, A., & Mazlish, E. (2012). *How to talk so kids will listen & listen so kids will talk* (Rev. ed.). Scribner.

Gladieux, M. (2020). *Communicate with courage: Taking risks to overcome the four hidden challenges.* Per Capita Publishing.

Goleman, D. (2006). *Social intelligence: The new science of human relationships.* Bantam Books.

Rock, D. (2010). Your brain at work: Strategies for overcoming distraction, regaining focus, and working smarter all day long. *Journal of Behavioral Optometry, 21*(5), 130.

Rosenberg, M. B. (2015). *Nonviolent communication: A language of life* (3rd ed.). PuddleDancer Press.

Turkle, S. (2016). *Reclaiming conversation: The power of talk in a digital age.* Penguin Books.

width:1103px; height:1697px;

Chapter 5: Confidence

Brown, B. (2021). *Atlas of the heart: Mapping meaningful connection and the language of human experience.* Random House.

Brown, B. (2018, March 13). Courage over comfort: Rumbling with shame, accountability, and failure at work. *Brené Brown Blog.* https://brenebrown.com/articles/2018/03/13/courage-comfort-rumbling-shame-accountability-failure-work

David, S. (2016). *Emotional agility: Get unstuck, embrace change, and thrive in work and life.* Avery.

Goleman, D. (1995). *Emotional intelligence: Why it can matter more than IQ.* Bantam Books.

Lerner, D., & Schlechter, A. (2017). *U thrive: How to succeed in college (and life).* Little, Brown Spark.

Marku, A. (2019). *The art of setting smart goals: 10 proven strategies to achieve anything you want in life.* Independently published.

McGonigal, K. (2015). *The upside of stress: Why stress is good for you, and how to get good at it.* Avery.

McKay, M., Wood, J. C., & Brantley, J. (2019). *The dialectical behavior therapy skills workbook: Practical DBT exercises for learning mindfulness, interpersonal effectiveness, emotion regulation and distress tolerance* (2nd ed.). New Harbinger Publications.

University of California, Office of the President. (2016). *SMART goals: A how-to guide.* https://www.ucop.edu/local-human-resources/_files/performance-appraisal/How+to+write+SMART+Goals+v2.pdf

The Wellbeing Lab. (n.d.). Learning loop. The Wellbeing Lab. https://www.michellemcquaid.com/

Chapter 6: Connection

Enright, R. D. (2001). *Forgiveness is a choice: A step-by-step process for resolving anger and restoring hope.* American Psychological Association.

Gable, S. L., Gonzaga, G. C., & Strachman, A. (2006). Will you be there for me when things go right? Supportive responses to positive event disclosures. *Journal of Personality and Social Psychology, 91*(5), 904–917.

Hood, K. (2021, October 13). *The benefits of active constructive responding.* Geelong Grammar School. https://www.ggs.vic.edu.au/2021/10/the-benefits-of-active-constructive-responding

Leahy, R. L. (2005). *The worry cure: Seven steps to stop worry from stopping you.* Harmony.

Luskin, F. (2002). *Forgive for good: A proven prescription for health and happiness.* HarperOne.

Morrison, B. (2005). Restorative justice in schools. In E. Elliott & R. M. Gordon (Eds.), *New directions in restorative justice* (pp. 26–52). Willan.

Murthy, V. H. (2020). *Together: The healing power of human connection in a sometimes lonely world.* Harper Wave.

Office of the Surgeon General. (2023). *Our epidemic of loneliness and isolation: The U.S. Surgeon General's advisory on the healing effects of social connection and community.* U.S. Department of Health and Human Services.

RSA. (2013, December 10). *Brené Brown on empathy* [Video]. YouTube. https://www.youtube.com/watch?v=1Evwgu369Jw

Shore, J. (2023). *Setting boundaries that stick: How neurobiology can help you rewire your brain to feel safe, connected, and empowered.* New Harbinger Publications.

Wiseman, T. (1996). A concept analysis of empathy. *Journal of Advanced Nursing, 23*(6), 1162–1167.

Worthington, E. L., Jr. (2006). *Forgiveness and reconciliation: Theory and application.* Routledge.

Part III: Purpose. Motivation. Intention

Chapter 7: Purpose

Brown, B. (2018). *Dare to lead.* Random House.

Cook-Deegan, P. (2015, April 16). *How to help teens find purpose.* Greater Good Science Center. https://greatergood.berkeley.edu/article/item/how_to_help_teens_find_purpose

Damon, W. (2008). *The path to purpose: Helping our children find their calling in life.* Free Press.

Finlay, A., Wray-Lake, L., Warren, M., & Maggs, J. L. (2015). Anticipating their future: Adolescent values for the future predict adult behaviors. *International Journal of Behavioral Development, 39*(4), 359–367. https://doi.org/10.1177/0165025414544231

Frankl, V. E. (2006). *Man's search for meaning* (I. Lasch, Trans.). Beacon Press. (Original work published 1946).

Fulghum, R. (1989). *All I really need to know I learned in kindergarten.* Villard Books.

Gamage, K., Dehideniya, D., & Ekanayake, S. (2021). The role of personal values in learning approaches and student achievements. *Behavioral Sciences, 11*(7), 102. https://doi.org/10.3390/bs11070102

Kabat-Zinn, J. (2012). *Mindfulness for beginners: Reclaiming the present moment and your life.* Sounds True.

Oeschger, T., Makarova, E., & Döring, A. K. (2022). Values in the school curriculum from teachers' perspective: A mixed-methods study. *International Journal of Educational Research Open, 3*, 100190. https://doi.org/10.1016/j.ijedro.2022.100190

Oishi, S., & Diener, E. (2014). Residents of poor nations have a greater sense of meaning in life than residents of wealthy nations. *Psychological Science, 25*(2), 422–430.

Prilleltensky, I., & Prilleltensky, O. (2021). *How people matter: Why it affects health, happiness, love, work, and society.* Cambridge University Press.

Random Acts of Kindness Foundation. (n.d.). *Random acts of kindness.* https://www.randomactsofkindness.orgRath, T. (2020). *Life's great question: Discover how you contribute to the world.* Silicon Guild.

Seligman, M. E. P. (2002). *Authentic happiness: Using the new positive psychology to realize your potential for lasting fulfillment.* Free Press.

Sutton, J. (2022, July). *Why is mindfulness important?* PositivePsychology.com. https://positivepsychology.com/importance-of-mindfulnessStopBullying.gov. (n.d.). *Get help now.* U.S. Department of Health and Human Services. https://www.stopbullying.gov/resources/get-help-now

Taberner, K., & Siggins, K. T. (2015). *The power of curiosity: How to have real conversations that create collaboration, innovation and understanding.* Morgan James Publishing.

Chapter 8: Motivation

Barger, T. (2023, January). The science of forming healthy habits. *Discover Magazine.*

Clear, J. (2018). *Atomic habits: An easy and proven way to build good habits and break bad ones.* Avery.

Csikszentmihalyi, M. (2008). *Flow: The psychology of optimal experience.* Harper Perennial Modern Classics.

Daniel, J. (2018). *Metacognition: A practical guide for educators.* Routledge.

Deci, E. L., & Ryan, R. M. (1985). *Intrinsic motivation and self-determination in human behavior.* Plenum.

Fogg, B. J. (2019). *Tiny habits: The small changes that change everything.* Houghton Mifflin Harcourt.

Greenwood, V. (n.d.). *The power of habit.* The Washington Center for Cognitive Therapy. https://washingtoncenterforcognitivetherapy.com/the-power-of-habitMcNally, M. (2023, October). Empower your mind: The power of choice. *Psychology Today.*

Newport, C. (2019). *Digital minimalism: Choosing a focused life in a noisy world.* Portfolio/Penguin.

Raihan, N., & Cogburn, M. (2023). Stages of change theory. In *StatPearls.* StatPearls Publishing. https://www.ncbi.nlm.nih.gov/books/NBK556005/

Reeve, J., Ryan, S., Cohen, G., Matos, L., & Kaplan, H. (2022). *Supporting students' motivation: Strategies for success.* Routledge.

Ryan, R. M. (Ed.). (2012). *The Oxford handbook of self-determination theory.* Oxford University Press.

Schwartz, B. (2004). *The paradox of choice: Why more is less.* Harper Perennial.

Center for Self-Determination Theory. (n.d.). *What is self-determination theory?* https://selfdeterminationtheory.org/theorySeligman, M. E. P. (2011). *Flourish: A visionary new understanding of happiness and well-being.* Free Press.

Sollisch, J. (2021, June). The cure for decision fatigue. *Wall Street Journal.* https://www.wsj.com/articles/the-cure-for-decision-fatigue-11625339514

Chapter 9: Intention

Bluth, K. (2017). *The self-compassion workbook for teens: Mindfulness and compassion skills to overcome self-criticism and embrace who you are.* New Harbinger Publications.

Collaborative for Academic, Social, and Emotional Learning (CASEL). (n.d.). https://casel.orgLa Torre, C. (2019). *The CBT workbook for perfectionism: Evidence-based skills to help you let go of self-criticism, build self-esteem, and find balance.* New Harbinger Publications.

Neff, K. D. (2011). The science of self-compassion. In C. K. Germer & R. D. Siegel (Eds.), *Compassion and wisdom in psychotherapy* (pp. 79–92). Guilford Press.

Steinberg, L. (2014). *Age of opportunity: Lessons from the new science of adolescence.* Eamon Dolan/Houghton Mifflin Harcourt.

Zins, J. E., Weissberg, R. P., Wang, M. C., & Walberg, H. J. (Eds.). (2004). *Building academic success on social and emotional learning: What does the research say?* Teachers College Press.

Evidence-Based Frameworks

Collaborative for Academic, Social, and Emotional Learning (CASEL). (2025). *Fundamentals of SEL.* https://casel.org/fundamentals-of-selThe Legacy Center for Community Success. (n.d.). *Past projects.* https://www.tlc4cs.org/projects/

McQuaid, M., & Kern, P. (2017). *Your wellbeing blueprint: Feeling good and doing well at work.* Victoria, Australia: McQuaid Ltd.

National Center for School Mental Health. (n.d.). Mental health promotion for all (Tier 1). University of Maryland School of Medicine. https://www.schoolmentalhealth.org/resources/mental-health-promotion-for-all-tier-1Positive Psychology Center. (n.d.). *Home.* University of Pennsylvania. Retrieved June 8, 2025, from https://ppc.sas.upenn.eduPositive Psychology Center. (n.d.). *PERMA™ theory of well-being and PERMA™ workshops.* University of Pennsylvania. https://ppc.sas.upenn.edu/learn-more/perma-theory-well-being-and-perma-workshops

Search Institute. (2017, February 9). *New research report: Relationships first—creating connections that help young people thrive.* https://blog.searchinstitute.org/new-research-report

Search Institute. (2025). *Developmental assets.* https://searchinstitute.org/developmental-assets

Search Institute. (2025). *Developmental relationships.* https://searchinstitute.org/developmental-relationships

Acknowledgments

Professionally, I would like to give special thanks to all the dedicated volunteers, board members, and staff of The ROCK and Discover You™ who, over the years, have made the vision of positively impacting youth a continued reality. Additionally, to all the partnering organizations, wise individuals, and friends who have personally influenced me, as well as the organization.

Personally, I want to thank my husband, Kevin, who has supported me, my work, and our family throughout the years. I also want to thank my son Thomas, who introduced me to The ROCK, and my daughter Nichole, who has always embraced the vision.

Most importantly, thank you to all the young people who have left an often joyful and occasionally heartbreaking imprint on my soul.

The ROCK and Discover You™

Reaching Our Community Kids has such a tale to share with you. That is the organization's legal name; however, it is better known in the Great Lakes Bay Region of Michigan as The ROCK Center for Youth Development. The ROCK is a not-for-profit 501(c)(3) impact organization that supports two major priorities: out-of-school-time, often called The ROCK OST, and Discover You™.

The ROCK story began in 2001 as a budding organization that prioritized out-of-school programs for middle and high school students. Over the years, tens of thousands of young people played a role in crafting this rich and impactful tale. Witnessing tremendous benefits being gained by young people, the focus expanded to intentionally building assets in youth. The ROCK's leaders released their first program in 2010, which became Discover You™ in 2014, as a means to exponentially develop assets in youth.

The impact of Discover You™ has been tremendous, with hundreds of adults trained to be Discover You™ coaches, delivering Discover You™ workshops and providing experiential learning directly to youth under their influence. In addition to the Discover You™ training program, thousands of adults nationwide have been served, supported, and trained through professional development and workshops.

Discover You™ is in schools, out-of-school programs, youth sports groups, and wherever youth are. The model is easily integrated into any setting where youth are resourced with caring adults committed to intentionally helping them build assets, such as resilience, hope, courage, and critical thinking. The ROCK OST serves youth at multiple locations throughout the school year and offers summer day camps. All OST programs are engaging, innovative, and productive. The participants often do not realize they are gaining life skills because they are highly engaged and having fun. In addition to Discover You™ concepts woven throughout, youth are learning life skills, including STEM, art, teamwork, literacy, and social skills. They also receive homework support, engage in physical activities, and enjoy meals. The ROCK OST has provided the foundation for the Discover You™ program and this book.

The ROCK's mission is to build hope and resilience in youth based on a foundation of acceptance, support, and respect. The vision is that all youth have the opportunity to live their potential.

The book *Discover Youth* is a compilation of The ROCK and Discover You™'s story. All proceeds from this book go to further the mission of The ROCK and Discover You™.

About the Author

Everyone has a story. I do not have a biography, but I do have a story similar to *Discover You*th; it is a compilation of years of experience and knowledge acquisition.

Because I was extremely curious, education always came quickly for me when I was interested; however, as I was also fiercely independent and easily bored, it failed to hold my attention for long. University followed high school graduation, but that only lasted a few years. Always having a knack for leading people, I became a restaurant manager at 18, though the primary qualification for that job was consistently showing up for work, which I did; thus, I got to be in charge. That illusion of success quickly diminished the need or interest to pursue a traditional degree.

In my early years, I worked in middle management, leading teams in various establishments, including restaurants and retail. I managed front-end departments, bakeries, delis, and entire stores. I acquired many skills along that path, including the ability to decorate a pretty nice cake for most occasions, direct you to natural remedies or herbs that can offset various ailments, efficiently operate a cash register, and make a mean pastrami sandwich. One of the key lessons I learned in retail that would serve me throughout life was social intelligence. It taught me how to understand people's needs, create an environment where diverse teams with conflicting priorities can thrive, and manage resources effectively.

I became a volunteer firefighter when I could no longer ignore the persistent yet nagging urge to rush into a burning building. This role achieved many objectives, including operating a 15-ton vehicle equipped with lights and sirens. I relished being in situations where people required clear, decisive problem-solvers who could act quickly and concisely. This situation led me to become a Medical First Responder (MFR), as my crew was generally the first on the scene of accidents. We were in a rural area, and medical help could be 15 minutes away. When one minute can often determine life or death, 15 seconds is an eternity.

Once I was able to be somewhat helpful as an MFR, I decided I needed more training to truly assist folks, so I became an Emergency Medical Technician (EMT). This fulfilled another dream of mine: to help people in extreme situations and ideally contribute to securing a positive outcome for them. Plus, I got to drive an ambulance. During this phase of my life, I learned that people live in harsh conditions and face impossible challenges, some in homes with dirt floors, broken windows, and no heat in areas that endure temperatures below 0 degrees F. When called to an emergency, there is no time to clean, prepare, pretend, or rehearse. You see people in their rawest states, and if you are a fortunate EMT, you develop empathy and compassion, which knows no bounds. I also discovered that I could do hard things, manage chaotic situations, and bring a sense of calm to even the most dire circumstances.

During all this, I became a single mom with two teens, then entered a blended situation with three teens and one young adult. All life is complex, with divorce, single parenting, and blended families adding another layer of complications and intricacies. Throughout that, I learned how little I actually knew about the challenges many families were facing, and that there is no one easy solution.

What do all these skills lead to? Well, running a nonprofit teen center, of course. It was the only logical outcome.

Once I began at The ROCK, I learned what I didn't know. That included things like understanding how a nonprofit differs from a for-profit, the fact that there was no money, and that it was my job to secure it. That one caught me by surprise. And wait, you can't get the money from the people you provide services to because they don't have any. This was unlike any for-profit business plan I had known. Those gaps, combined with a relentless need to ensure The ROCK thrived on my watch, led me to attend the Michigan Nonprofit Executive Leadership Fellows, a year-long immersive experience designed to teach me how to lead a nonprofit. There, I gathered information to understand the nuances of this enigma for which I was now responsible.

That complete, the financial aspect was still a looming beast. I spent several years honing my fundraising skills with the Lilly Family School of Philanthropy at Indiana University. What I learned there was how to raise money ethically and that not all fundraisers are ethical.

Eventually, I attended Saginaw Valley State University to become a Certified Public Manager. That adventure helped lay a foundation for more impactful community and state-level work.

The Flourishing Lab provided me with a certificate in Wellbeing, and the Master of Applied Positive Psychology department of the University of Pennsylvania allowed me the opportunity to partner with three different classes as service-learning projects. Working with the Michelle McQuaid team in Australia, I co-created the Certificate in Creating Wellbeing and the Certificate in Applied Positive Psychology, both of which are available worldwide.

All this contributed to the creation of Discover You™ and the book *Discover Youth: A Comprehensive Guide to Equip and Inspire Adults Who Impact Youth*. This primary publication is supported by a series of Discovery Journals: *Hope. Strength. Resilience.; Courage. Confidence. Connection.*; and *Purpose. Motivation. Intention.*

My name is Beverlee Wenzel, and I served as President and CEO of The ROCK from 2003, when The ROCK was two years old, through 2024. And the tale continues...

If you are curious, my signature character strengths have fluctuated over the years, but they predominantly consist of humor, creativity, gratitude, hope, and curiosity, with perspective, social intelligence, zest, and bravery being interwoven. My lesser, and I mean lesser, strengths are prudence and self-regulation. DISC describes me as a strong D, and CliftonStrengths™ says I'm a strategic thinker. Oh, and I am a Sagittarius to a ridiculous level, so just read the horoscopes to see how my world is going. The next chapter is still unfolding. I expect to continue speaking, facilitating, consulting, and writing. I will wholeheartedly enjoy my adult children and their families, especially as a grandmother. I look forward to traveling, doing all the crafts I've been buying supplies for, and spending evenings on the beach watching the sunset with my husband.